Hope in a Time of Chaos and Evil:
The Message of the Book of Revelation for Today

HOPE
in a Time of
CHAOS
and EVIL

*The Message of
the Book of Revelation
for Today*

by
David A. Palmer

PLACE TO GROW
PRESS
2018

Printed in the United States of America

First Printing, 2018

ISBN 978-1-7321245-0-9

Place to Grow Press
1435 East Main Street
Kent, OH 44240

www.KentMethodist.org

CONTENTS

FOREWORD

There is no Biblical book more misunderstood and abused than the book of Revelation. Although there is solid scholarly consensus on how the book is to be read, that consensus has been buried for many years by an avalanche of popular distortions and prognostications that people have spun out of the visions of Revelation. The average Christian is left with false ideas about the book or a desire to avoid the book altogether!

Yet the book of Revelation has a direct and powerful message for our time, a message that brings real encouragement for all who would despair over the troubles and threats of the present age.

This volume will guide the reader through the major visions of Revelation, noting how the imagery has often been abused, and how these visions are rightly understood. The reader will find that the book of Revelation has a very pertinent message for our own time—a message of hope within a time of chaos and evil.

THE APOCALYPSE
REVELATION CHAPTER 1A

The apocalypse [revelation] of Jesus Christ, which God gave him to show his servants what must soon take place; he made it known by sending his angel to his servant John, who testified to the word of God and to the testimony of Jesus Christ, even to all that he saw.

Blessed is the one who reads aloud the words of the prophecy, and blessed are those who hear and who keep what is written in it; for the time is near. John to the seven churches that are in Asia: Grace to you and peace from him who is and who was and who is to come, and from the seven spirits who are before his throne, and from Jesus Christ, the faithful witness, the firstborn of the dead, and the ruler of the kings of the earth. To him who loves us and freed us from our sins by his blood, and made us to be a kingdom, priests serving his God and Father, to him be glory and dominion forever and ever. Amen. Look! He is coming with the clouds; every eye will see him, even those who pierced him; and on his account all the tribes of the earth will wail. So it is to be. Amen. "I am the Alpha and the Omega," says the Lord God, who is and who was and who is to come, the Almighty.

I, John, your brother who share with you in Jesus the persecution and the kingdom and the patient endurance, was on the island called Patmos because of the word of God and the testimony of Jesus.

Revelation 1:1–9

In March of 2018, as Syrian bombs rained on besieged rebels in eastern Ghouta, destroying hospitals and claiming the lives of countless civilians, U.N. human rights chief Zeid Ra'ad Al Hussein decried the wholesale destruction of Ghouta and other places in Syria as *an apocalypse.*[i] In common usage today, the word "apocalypse" indicates cataclysmic devastation. Thus in 1979 a movie depicting ruinous destruction in the Vietnam War was entitled "Apocalypse Now."

The book of Revelation begins, "The apocalypse of Jesus Christ…" (Revelation 1:1). What follows in the book is a series of very startling scenes, some of which depict sweeping devastations upon the earth. It is from these images of destruction that the word "apocalypse" gets its contemporary meaning; and many readers of the last book in the Bible expect that this book will be all about a set of devastating judgments that God is going to send upon the earth.

Yet in its original form the word "apocalypse" — in Greek, ἀποκάλυψις or *apokálypsis* — does not indicate any sort of calamity. The word actually means *revelation.* This is why the first verse is typically translated, "The revelation of Jesus Christ…" and what follows is appropriately called the book of Revelation. Modern readers are wrongly predisposed if they approach this book assuming that it must be about coming calamities to be ushered in by Christ. The book at the outset tells us quite simply that it is a *revelation of God's truth.*

Christians understand the entire Bible to be revelation — a communication of God's truth to humankind — and thus the "book of Revelation" is the capstone of the whole story of God's self-revelation. What makes this book different from the

3

revelation that unfolds through the rest of the Scripture is the style of the book, as Revelation contains a series of very dramatic and ofttimes strange images. In Biblical studies, this style is called *apocalyptic writing.*

Verse one of Revelation goes on to note that the book was written by a man named John, which was a very common name at the time. This was not John the disciple, who is believed to have written the gospel and the letters of John. The gospel and the letters of John are very similar to one another in style and vocabulary, but the book of Revelation is quite different from them all, not only in content but in its use of the Greek language. It was clearly written by a different hand. The John of Revelation was another leader in the early church, who was exiled for his faith to the island of Patmos. There is a cave on the island that is the traditional site where he wrote the book of Revelation, although no one knows if he really spent any time there! One possibility is that the writer of Revelation was "John the Elder," a prominent church leader who is referenced in ancient church documents. The one thing that is certain about him is that he was living during a time of great challenge for Christians in the late first century.

Sometimes when people read the book of Revelation, they think that John was writing down mystical visions. They imagine him in his cave, caught up in a visionary trance, scribbling down surreal images cascading through his mind. Many a modern reader has asked, "What was he smoking?" Yet this would be to completely misunderstand what was happening when John wrote!

When John engaged in apocalyptic writing, he was using a literary style that had become widespread in Jewish circles since the second century BC. There were numerous apocalyptic titles, and John's audience would have been familiar with how to read the apocalyptic genre. The apocalyptic style often dealt with the problem of rampant evil in the world, and it used striking images to convey a message about what God is doing, or what God will do, in response. As bizarre as the images might appear to the modern reader, they were very familiar images to the original readers. Virtually all of the images in Revelation are drawn from the cultural and religious setting of the time.

John was not jotting down strange visions. He was making careful use of imagery that would plainly communicate with his readers. In employing the apocalyptic style, his work was something like that of an artist. He conceived images that would resonate with his audience, and he put those to paper.

This does not mean that what he wrote was not a revelation of God's truth. Early Christians perceived that John was inspired by God to write, in the same way that God had inspired other Biblical writers. John sensed a message from God, and he expressed that message, under God's leading, in a book that would come to be recognized as Scripture. The difference between John and other Biblical writers is that while they wrote in prose or poetry, he wrote with apocalyptic imagery.

This means that John knew exactly what he was saying. His visions do not have meanings that were waiting to be unlocked by preachers and prognosticators twenty centuries later. To understand the visions, one needs to look at what the imagery *actually meant* for John and his original audience. When this is done, the meaning of the imagery becomes clear; and the modern reader will find that for all their strangeness, the images bring a powerful message for the modern world — a world in which evil again is rampant, and for which there is a message of real hope from God.

A MESSAGE FOR THE PRESENT DAY
REVELATION CHAPTER 1B

I was in the spirit on the Lord's day, and I heard behind me a loud voice like a trumpet saying, "Write in a book what you see and send it to the seven churches, to Ephesus, to Smyrna, to Pergamum, to Thyatira, to Sardis, to Philadelphia, and to Laodicea." Then I turned to see whose voice it was that spoke to me, and on turning I saw seven golden lampstands, and in the midst of the lampstands I saw one like the Son of Man, clothed with a long robe and with a golden sash across his chest. His head and his hair were white as white wool, white as snow; his eyes were like a flame of fire, his feet were like burnished bronze, refined as in a furnace, and his voice was like the sound of many waters. In his right hand he held seven stars, and from his mouth came a sharp, two-edged sword, and his face was like the sun shining with full force. When I saw him, I fell at his feet as though dead. But he placed his right hand on me, saying, "Do not be afraid; I am the first and the last, and the living one. I was dead, and see, I am alive forever and ever; and I have the keys of Death and of Hades. Now write what you have seen, what is, and what is to take place after this. As for the mystery of the seven stars that you saw in my right hand, and the seven golden lampstands: the seven stars are the angels of the seven churches, and the seven lampstands are the seven churches."

Revelation 1:10–20

In 1988, a former NASA engineer by the name of Edgar Whisenant created a national sensation by predicting that the Rapture—when faithful Christians would be whisked out of the world before the final end times—would occur in September of 1988, on Rosh Hashanah, which would put the date of the Rapture at no later than September 13, 1988. He wrote a book entitled, *88 Reasons Why the Rapture Will Be in 1988,* which sold 4.3 million copies. The Trinity Broadcasting Network began giving instructions on how to prepare for the Rapture. As the date approached, a TV station in Raleigh, North Carolina, reported that believers there were selling their cars and boats in order to prepare for the end. You won't need a car and boat if you are about to be transported to heaven! Of course, neither will you need the proceeds from the sale of a car or boat. What exactly were these believers thinking? In any case, they took Whisenant's predictions with the utmost seriousness. Yet September 13 passed without incident, whereupon Whisenant hastily adjusted his date to a day later, to account, he said, for the International Date Line; but nothing happened then either. He subsequently wrote another book, entitled, *The Final Shot: Rapture Report 1989,* in which he announced a new and improved prediction of Sep. 1, 1989. Two more books followed, moving the date to 1993 and then 1994. Sales steadily declined. Whisenant finally decided to retire from end-of-the-world predicting; but, he said, "I can stand in front of the Lord and say I gave it my best shot."

History is full of Edgar Whisenants—people who have used the Bible, and the book of Revelation in particular, to try to predict the end of the world. In the 1840's, William Miller used passages from Revelation and elsewhere in the Bible to predict the second coming of Christ in 1843; and he gathered a considerable following. When nothing happened in 1843, he extended the date to 1844, a typical pattern in end-of-the-world predicting. He and his followers finally landed on the date of October 22, 1844. Thousands of believers went to hilltops that night in white robes, waiting for Christ to return in glory. The whole thing was subsequently dubbed "The Great Disappointment."

This, however, did not put an end to attempts to predict "the end times." In the late nineteenth century, Charles Taze Russell, again with many references to the book of Revelation, predicted that the present age would end in 1914. When World War I broke out, it seemed perhaps to support his prediction, but of course history rolled on. Nevertheless, Russell's followers, the Jehovah's Witnesses, insisted that the 1914 date was valid and that it was the *beginning* of the end; they subsequently taught that the generation alive in 1914 would not completely pass away before the Second Coming occurs. They have pretty much run out of time. In recent years, the Jehovah's Witnesses have begun to redefine what exactly a "generation" is.

Many people have taken a shot at predicting the Second Coming and the end of the age; and every shot has been a complete miss.

One might think that people would learn something from this. The problem with end-of-the-world predictors is not simply that they have miscalculated, as though maybe the next prediction will finally hit the mark. The problem is that all these people have approached the book of Revelation in completely the wrong way.

Often people have wanted to treat the book of Revelation as though it were a set of secret, coded predictions of the future. Their assumption is that the book had no real reference to the first century when it was written, and that the images are all mysterious predictions of events that are now unfolding in our time. With this assumption, the standard approach of "end-times" writers and preachers is to take verses and images from here and there in the Bible — especially from the book of Revelation — and to try to line them up with present day events. The result is an unending series of "last days" scenarios and predictions. But this whole approach distorts and misuses the Bible, because it ignores what the Bible itself actually says.

The book of Revelation states in the first chapter who the intended recipients of the book were. The book is a letter, addressed in verse 11 not to modern end-times predictors but to seven first-century churches. There follows a list of seven actual first-century churches: Ephesus, Smyrna, Pergamum, Thyatira, Sardis, Philadelphia, and Laodicea. They are listed in the order in which a courier would have traveled from one church to another. Chapters two and three will contain specific admonitions for each of the churches. What is clear at the outset is that the book of Revelation was speaking to these Christians and their situation in the first century. In order to understand the book, it is essential to do what one would do in understanding any letter—one must understand the circumstance of the original audience.

The book of Revelation was written in the late first century; most scholars place it in 95–96 AD. For Christians, this was a time of mounting persecution. Persecution against Christians directed by Rome had actually started under Emperor Nero in the 60's. After Nero, persecution waned; but in the 80's and 90's, under Emperor Domitian, the persecution resumed, as Domitian revived and pressed the imperial cult—the worship of the emperor as an expression of submission to the empire. Domitian insisted that everyone in the empire must address him as *dominus et deus noster*—"our lord and god." All people in the empire were expected to offer worship to the Romans gods, including the emperor, as a sign of loyalty. Those who refused could be tortured and brutally executed.

Jews were exempt from this requirement, since it was known that their ancient religion precluded offering sacrifices to idols, and Romans had a respect for ancient practice. In the early part of the first century, Christians had been considered a movement within Judaism; but by the latter part of the century, Christians were distinct from the Jewish synagogues. Roman authorities confronting the new movement were often not quite sure what to make of Christians; but if anything, Christianity appeared to be an upstart and potentially dangerous movement. If its followers refused to sacrifice to the Roman gods and the emperor, this seemed proof that they were guilty of rebellion and that they were disseminating ideas that would undermine Roman society.

Christians found themselves hauled before magistrates. How this unfolded varied regionally. There was not yet an aggressive empire-wide persecution — that would come later. Persecutions were often spurred by zealous locals, and judgments varied according to regional rulers.

In 112 AD, Pliny the Younger, a Roman magistrate, was sent to govern the Roman province of Bithynia-Pontus, located in what is now northern Turkey. Pliny wrote a letter to the emperor Trajan in which he said, "In the case of those who were denounced to me as Christians, I have observed the following procedure: I interrogated these as to whether they were Christians; those who confessed I interrogated a second and a third time, threatening them with punishment; those who persisted I ordered executed.... Those who denied that they were or had been Christians, when they invoked the gods in words dictated by me, offered prayer with incense and wine to your image, which I had ordered to be brought for this purpose together with statues of the gods, and moreover cursed Christ, these I thought should be discharged."[ii] Pliny went on to inform Trajan that some people confessed that they had once been Christians, but they had renounced the faith, and "They all worshipped your image and the statues of the gods, and cursed Christ." He added that he tried to find out more about the actual beliefs and practices of Christians "by torturing two female slaves who were called deaconesses." Since Pliny was new at this, he was seeking the emperor's guidance as to whether he was following the proper procedures. Trajan replied, "You observed proper procedure, my dear Pliny."[iii]

The seven churches to which the book of Revelation was addressed were in the Roman province of Asia, directly adjacent to and just southwest of Bithynia-Pontus. It is likely that circumstances there were very similar to what Pliny described. Christians were being put on trial on the charge of being Christian. They had to curse Christ and offer worship to the Roman gods and emperor—or die.

It was to these Christians that the book of Revelation was explicitly addressed; and it brought to them not a set of mysteriously coded predictions that were waiting to be decoded by end-times predictors twenty centuries later; it brought them a powerful message for their time, a message that would bring them great encouragement.

What was the message? The message in the book of Revelation is expressed in visions, a very rich set of word pictures. It is very important to recognize how these images were originally experienced by the first recipients of the book. In the opening of the book, John says, "Blessed is the one who reads aloud the words of the prophecy, and blessed are those who hear and who keep what is written in it." (Revelation 1:3) When the book of Revelation was taken to each of the seven churches to which it was addressed, it was read aloud before the whole congregation. People experienced the book by hearing it. This means that they did not dwell on each detail but encountered each vision in its totality as it was sketched before them. This points to how the book of Revelation should be experienced today! The book is designed not so much for rational analysis of each verse; it is best experienced in the way that one would journey through the paintings in an art gallery—seeing each image in its totality, feeling the overall impact of each painting. In Revelation, one could become entangled in lengthy discussions about all the details; but the book becomes most fruitful when one reflects about each vision as a whole.

The Harvard Biblical scholar Elisabeth Schussler Fiorenza described how the apocalyptic style in this book should be experienced when she said that the book of Revelation "seeks to persuade and motivate by constructing a 'symbolic universe' that invites imaginative participation. The strength of its persuasion for action lies not in theological reasoning or historical argument but in the evocative power of its symbols."[iv] The reader is to let the symbolic imagery speak deeply to the soul.

The vision in the last part of chapter one makes a profound statement when viewed in this way. It is a vision of Christ (the "Son of Man") in which the elements are clearly not meant to be understood literally, but they convey a powerful sense of the glorious character of Christ. The white hair calls to mind the ancient origin of Christ, the feet like burnished bronze give a feeling of stability and strength, and the face shining like the sun gives a sense of great goodness and might. The sword issuing from the mouth recalls the Biblical statement that the word of God is like a sharp, two-edged sword (Hebrews 4:12). Here it is significant that the sword of Christ is not in his hand, as though he exercises a violent power, but in his mouth, which is to say that the power of Christ is expressed through his *word*.

Most significantly, the figure of Christ stands among seven lampstands, which are said to represent the seven churches to which the book was addressed. The message of this for the original hearers of the book was clear. It may seem, the vision told them, that the emperor is all-powerful. But beyond the emperor there is a greater power; there is more to reality than what first meets the eye, because beyond the empire there is the true power of the universe—the Lord—and the Lord stands with the churches.

The impact of this message for those first Christians was profound. The book of Revelation said to them: "You are surrounded by threats, but you do not need to be afraid or give in, because the Lord, the real strength of the universe, is in your midst. Hold on to your faith in Christ!" It is precisely on this level that the vision in Revelation can speak to Christians today. The vision of Christ in glory does not bring predictions of the future; but *it speaks in the same way that it spoke to the Christians in the first century.* The vision says to today's Christians: You may be facing tremendous evils and pressures, and it may seem that trouble has the upper hand; but do not be afraid, do not lose hope! The Lord is greater than any trial, the Lord is greater even than death, and the Lord stands with you. Hold on to your faith in Christ.

The book of Revelation brings a message for today—not because the book contains predictions or timetables for modern people to decipher, but because the book speaks a message that applies to the present age as much as it did to the first century. The book was written to bring a message of hope for people in rough times. If you find yourself facing challenges in life, then this is a book written for you; for it brings encouraging news from the One who said, "Fear not, I am the first and the last; I died, and behold I am alive for evermore." (Revelation 1:17–18)

WHAT THE SPIRIT SAYS TO THE CHURCHES
REVELATION CHAPTERS 2 AND 3

"And to the angel of the church in Philadelphia write: These are the words of the holy one, the true one, who has the key of David, who opens and no one will shut, who shuts and no one opens:

"I know your works. Look, I have set before you an open door, which no one is able to shut. I know that you have but little power, and yet you have kept my word and have not denied my name. I will make those of the synagogue of Satan who say that they are Jews and are not, but are lying—I will make them come and bow down before your feet, and they will learn that I have loved you. Because you have kept my word of patient endurance, I will keep you from the hour of trial that is coming on the whole world to test the inhabitants of the earth. I am coming soon; hold fast to what you have, so that no one may seize your crown. If you conquer, I will make you a pillar in the temple of my God; you will never go out of it. I will write on you the name of my God, and the name of the city of my God, the new Jerusalem that comes down from my God out of heaven, and my own new name. Let anyone who has an ear listen to what the Spirit is saying to the churches.

"And to the angel of the church in Laodicea write: The words of the Amen, the faithful and true witness, the origin of God's creation:

"I know your works; you are neither cold nor hot. I wish that you were either cold or hot. So, because you are lukewarm, and neither cold nor hot, I am about to spit you out of my mouth. For you say, 'I am rich, I have prospered, and I need nothing.' You do not realize that you are wretched, pitiable, poor, blind, and naked. Therefore I counsel you to buy from me gold refined by fire so that you may be rich; and white robes to clothe you and to keep the shame of your nakedness from being seen; and salve to anoint your eyes so that you may see. I reprove and discipline those whom I love. Be earnest, therefore, and repent. Listen! I am standing at the door, knocking; if you hear my voice and open the door, I will come in to you and eat with you, and you with me. To the one who conquers I will give a place with me on my throne, just as I myself conquered and sat down with my Father on his throne. Let anyone who has an ear listen to what the Spirit is saying to the churches."

Revelation 3:7–22

A tourist driving through west Texas stopped at a gas station where he noticed a dangling piece of rope with sign above it that said "Weather Forecaster." He asked the attendant, "How on earth do you expect to tell the weather from that piece of rope?" "Quite simple," said the attendant. "When the rope swings back and forth, it's windy. When it's wet, it's raining. When it's stiff as a board, it's freezing. When it's gone … tornado."

Obviously, that gas station attendant was a little confused about his weather forecaster rope, since he was expecting it to tell him what the weather will be, whereas the rope was telling him what the weather *is*. There is a similar confusion in many people's minds about the book of Revelation. Many people expect that the whole thrust of the book of Revelation is to speak of what will be in the future. The book of Revelation will indeed speak to the future; but the book speaks first of all to *what is* in the first century. This is clear in Revelation chapter one, when John is instructed, "Write what you have seen — what is, and what is to come." (Revelation 1:19) The emphasis on "what is" appears in the central vision of the first chapter — a vision of Christ in power and glory, standing *right now* among the believers in the first-century churches. The accent on present spiritual realities — from the perspective of the first century — continues in chapters two and three.

These chapters contain a series of admonitions directed to seven churches in western Asia Minor (modern-day Turkey). In each case, the Lord begins by saying to the congregation, "I know your works," and there follows a detailed discussion of what each church is doing and even what certain individuals in the church are doing. There is a clear sense that Christ knows every church and every member intimately.

It is easy for people to imagine that in God's sight they simply blend into the crowd. There are two billion Christians in the world. Surely, one thinks, God does not have a particular eye on me! But the book of Revelation communicates something quite different. "I know your works," the Lord says. (Revelation 2:2, and verses following) This can perhaps be an unsettling thought—that the Lord knows your every imperfection and failure. On the other hand, there is a very encouraging message here—that the Lord is personally interested in every single human being. Each person is of value to God, each person is understood by God; and God has the wisdom to guide each person on the right path. The way in which God specifically addresses people right where they are in life is powerfully illustrated in the various admonitions that are given to the seven churches in the Roman province of Asia.

The same pattern is found in all seven admonitions. The church's situation is precisely described, the church's struggle is identified, and in each case the Lord gives specific guidance, so that people in the congregation can be brought onto the right track. Often the situation described—and the counsel given—can be seen to directly correspond with similar circumstances in churches today.

In the town of Philadelphia, for example, the congregation had been faithful to God, but the people now were suffering a good deal of persecution, particularly from a group of radical Jews in the synagogue. Here is an indication that the persecution of early Christians came not only from the Roman government but also from pockets of conservative Jews who despised the Christians and worked hand in hand with Roman persecutors. The reference in this passage to "the synagogue of Satan" (Revelation 3:9) is by no means intended to be anti-Semitic—the Christian church itself included many Jews as well as Gentiles—but it indicated the extreme evil of people who masqueraded as godly folks ("they say they are Jews but are not" Revelation 3:9) but who were persecuting the faithful.

In the face of such persecution, coming even from people who claimed to be godly, the Lord offered a message of great support. "Because you have kept my word of patient endurance," said the Lord, "I will keep you from the hour of trial." (Revelation 3:10) There is also a word of encouragement to hold on in faith — "Hold fast to what you have, so that no one may seize your crown." (Revelation 3:11) Surely this is a word of encouragement for Christians today who are being persecuted, sometimes by people who say they are acting for God!

Perhaps the most striking image in the message to the church at Philadelphia is when the Lord says, "Behold, I have set before you an open door, which no one is able to shut." (Revelation 3:8) God has opened for us the door to heaven! And no one has the power to shut us out. Overall, the word to Philadelphia is an enormous word of assurance for Christians who are in a time of trial.

While the church in Philadelphia received commendation and encouragement, in other settings the critique is sharper, and this was certainly the case in Laodicea. Of all the churches mentioned in the book of Revelation, the church in Laodicea was perhaps the most similar in situation to many American churches today. Laodicea was a sizeable town with a booming economy that specialized in banking, the manufacture of fine clothing, and the production of a popular eye salve. Business was going well, so that the people were living quite comfortably. Yet it was perhaps their very comfort which led to their spiritual problem. They were, the Lord says, *lukewarm*. They were not cold to God, but they were not exactly "on fire" either; they were just lukewarm. (Revelation 3:16)

In Laodicea, the Lord challenged Christians to come to a vital faith. It is significant that although these people were loaded with money and clothing and eye salve, the Lord said that they were in fact "poor, naked, and blind"; and the Lord said, "Come to me for gold and white garments and salve to anoint your eyes." (Revelation 3:17-18) In other words, one can find real life and genuine riches only by coming to a wholehearted commitment to Jesus Christ. Again, this is also a very relevant message for today!

In the admonitions to the rest of the seven churches, the Lord addresses a variety of other problems, which run the gamut of common church difficulties. It is interesting to observe that even the first Christians were still human and imperfect and subject to all manner of stumbling. One church suffered from moral laxity; another had a problem with doctrinal compromise—watering down true beliefs. One church had a problem with divisions in the church; people were not loving one another the way that they should. Still another was judged to be spiritually dead and was told to wake up, and another was urged not to shy away from trials. These were seven actual churches that were addressed; yet it may be significant that John chose seven churches, because for John the number seven is a number representing completeness or wholeness—since God created the whole world in seven days—and so it is likely that John meant for these churches to be representative of the whole church in every time.

Just as the troubles in these churches have parallels to today, so the messages of these passages in Revelation speak also to today. The overall message, along with the whole tone of these chapters, is summed up well in verse 19 of chapter 3, where the Lord says, "Those whom I love, I reprove and chasten, so repent and be zealous." If the Lord makes believers aware of errors in the church and weaknesses in their lives and calls for change, it is because of God's love and desire for people to find a good life; and so believers are encouraged to "repent"—turn to the Lord—and "be zealous"—find a life that is truly on fire with the Spirit of God.

Chapter three concludes with an image that has become one of the most beloved images in the book of Revelation. It is the image of the Lord standing at the door knocking. Here it is not the door of heaven, which stands open, but rather the door of human hearts and lives, which may be closed. Holman Hunt captured this beautifully in his famous painting, *The Light of the World*, where he portrayed a compassionate Christ knocking at a door; but the door had no latch on the outside—it had to be opened from within. In Revelation the Lord says, "If you hear my voice and open the door, I will come in to you..." (Revelation 3:20)

Here is a clear invitation to every person to let Christ enter in to shape and empower life.

Christians in the late first century, like Christians today, lived in a very challenging world. Those challenges are depicted graphically in the book of Revelation. Sometimes it was the hardships of life which caused people to falter in their faith. Sometimes it was the ease and good fortune of life which enticed people to drift in their faith. Sometimes people were tempted to fall into the moral laxity or the strange ideas of the surrounding culture. It all sounds familiar! In the midst of everything, the central image in Revelation chapters two and three is that *the Spirit of God is speaking to the churches.* All seven admonitions end with the phrase, "Let anyone who has an ear listen to what the Spirit is saying to the churches." (Revelation 3:22) Here is God's call to the church in every age — to listen to what God is saying so that today's believers may be drawn into a life of genuine faith.

THE ONE ON THE THRONE
REVELATION CHAPTERS 4 AND 5

After this I looked, and there in heaven a door stood open! And the first voice, which I had heard speaking to me like a trumpet, said, "Come up here, and I will show you what must take place after this." At once I was in the spirit, and there in heaven stood a throne, with one seated on the throne! And the one seated there looks like jasper and carnelian, and around the throne is a rainbow that looks like an emerald. Around the throne are twenty-four thrones, and seated on the thrones are twenty-four elders, dressed in white robes, with golden crowns on their heads. Coming from the throne are flashes of lightning, and rumblings and peals of thunder, and in front of the throne burn seven flaming torches, which are the seven spirits of God; and in front of the throne there is something like a sea of glass, like crystal. Around the throne, and on each side of the throne, are four living creatures, full of eyes in front and behind: the first living creature like a lion, the second living creature like an ox, the third living creature with a face like a human face, and the fourth living creature like a flying eagle.

And the four living creatures, each of them with six wings, are full of eyes all around and inside. Day and night without ceasing they sing, "Holy, holy, holy, the Lord God the Almighty, who was and is and is to come." And whenever the living creatures give glory and honor and thanks to the one who is seated on the throne, who lives forever and ever, the twenty-four elders fall before the one who is seated on the throne and worship the one who lives forever and ever; they cast their crowns before the throne, singing, "You are worthy, our Lord and God, to receive glory and honor and power, for you created all things, and by your will they existed and were created."

Revelation 4:1–11

Then I saw in the right hand of the one seated on the throne a scroll written on the inside and on the back, sealed with seven seals; and I saw a mighty angel proclaiming with a loud voice, "Who is worthy to open the scroll and break its seals?" And no one in heaven or on earth or under the earth was able to open the scroll or to look into it. And I began to weep bitterly because no one was found worthy to open the scroll or to look into it. Then one of the elders said to me, "Do not weep. See, the Lion of the tribe of Judah, the Root of David, has conquered, so that he can open the scroll and its seven seals."

Then I saw between the throne and the four living creatures and among the elders a Lamb standing as if it had been slaughtered, having seven horns and seven eyes, which are the seven spirits of God sent out into all the earth. He went and took the scroll from the right hand of the one who was seated on the throne. When he had taken the scroll, the four living creatures and the twenty-four elders fell before the Lamb, each holding a harp and golden bowls full of incense, which are the prayers of the saints. They sing a new song: "You are worthy to take the scroll and to open its seals, for you were slaughtered and by your blood you ransomed for God saints from every tribe and language and people and nation; you have made them to be a kingdom and priests serving our God, and they will reign on earth." Then I looked, and I heard the voice of many angels surrounding the throne and the living creatures and the elders; they numbered myriads of myriads and thousands of thousands, singing with full voice, "Worthy is the Lamb that was slaughtered to receive power and wealth and wisdom and might and honor and glory and blessing!" Then I heard every creature in heaven and on earth and under the earth and in the sea, and all that is in them, singing, "To the one seated on the throne and to the Lamb be blessing and honor and glory and might forever and ever!" And the four living creatures said, "Amen!" And the elders fell down and worshiped.

Revelation 5:1–14

In June of 1996, there was an outbreak of hysteria in Latin America over the expectation that the Antichrist would appear on June 6, 1996. The book of Revelation says that "the number of the beast is 666" (Revelation 13:18), and someone predicted on this basis that the Antichrist would come on the date of 6/6/96. In Columbia, thousands of people brought their children to church to have them baptized before the fateful day. In Lima, Peru, a group of Peruvian shamans entered a major hospital on June 6 in order to hold a ritual in the maternity area designed to ward off the Antichrist's arrival. According to a Reuter's news service report at the time, "Eight cloaked shamans from the Andes scattered petals around pregnant mothers, plunged knives into red devil dolls and danced around skulls, snails, goats' feet and snake skins to the astonishment of staff and patients." One nurse, when asked about the experience, commented, "Their chants and their loud maracas' sounds annoyed the pregnant women a bit."

She was a master of understatement. The whole event was one more example of how people have often reacted in a highly superstitious fashion to the book of Revelation. The imagery in Revelation has been given all manner of bizarre interpretation. This occurs in part because the imagery to many people is so obscure. In chapters four and five, for example, there are descriptions of four winged creatures with various faces, and a lamb with seven eyes and seven horns. It is perhaps little wonder that such strange imagery produces strange ideas!

Yet while the images in the book of Revelation may strike modern readers as bizarre and incomprehensible, to the Christians in the late first century, to whom the book of Revelation was addressed, the images were not at all strange. When early Christians read the book of Revelation, they readily understood it, because they read this kind of material all the time. The apocalyptic style used in Revelation was widespread, and was present also in some other Biblical books, such as Zechariah and major parts of Daniel.

The main characteristic of the apocalyptic style was the use of evocative imagery to convey a message. For example, in the book of II Esdras, which is in the Apocrypha (included in the Catholic Old Testament), there is a vision of an eagle with three heads and twelve wings, out of which some other wings grew, and then most of the wings disappeared, and then one of the heads disappeared, and then one of the two remaining heads ate the other one. (II Esdras chapter 11) This was standard fare for apocalyptic books, and there were scores of books in this style in circulation in the first century.

When first-century Christians encountered the fantastic images in the book of Revelation, they were on familiar ground. They had seen this kind of imagery before, and they knew what the images meant. Consider an analogy out of twenty-first century traffic patterns. When you drive down a road, you encounter a number of cryptic symbols, but you know immediately what they mean. You know what a green light means, you know what an orange cone means, and you know what a double yellow line means. If a first-century person were to suddenly appear on a twenty-first century road and were to attempt to navigate, it might all be quite mystifying. One would hope that such a person would do more than just speculate about what all these symbols could mean but would find out what the symbols do mean!

If modern Christians are to navigate successfully through the book of Revelation, it is essential to do more than speculate about the symbols. One must ask what the symbols actually meant for the people who used them!

In almost every case, the symbols in Revelation had a clear and immediate meaning for the first-century audience. Numbers, for example, in apocalyptic writing, have standard symbolic meanings. Chapter five speaks of 24 elders around the throne of God (Revelation 5:8). When early Christians saw any number that was a multiple of 12, they thought of 12 disciples or 12 tribes of Israel, so 12 as a number represented the people of God. 12 tribes of Israel plus 12 disciples is 24 — so the image of 24 elders is an image representing the whole people of God worshipping before God's throne. Chapter four speaks of 4 living creatures around the throne (Revelation 4:6). The number 4 in apocalyptic writing represents the earth, since there are four directions of north, south, east, and west. The chapter goes on to say that the creatures had faces — one like a lion, another like an ox, another like an eagle, and another like a human being (Revelation 4:7). In ancient times, the natural order was divided into four basic categories: wild animals (the lion), domesticated animals (the ox), birds (the eagle), and human beings. The image of these four creatures represented all of creation praising God.

One can get a sense here of how to read apocalyptic writing. The images are not meant to be understood literally, nor are they meant to be a launching point for wild speculation — they are intended to convey a definite message to the reader. So one might ask, Why not just express the message in a straightforward way instead of through all these wild images? The answer is that a picture is worth a thousand words. A gripping image can communicate with more profound impact than conceptual words alone. The writer of Revelation could have simply said, "God is in charge, and all of creation and all God's people praise God." This is the basic message of chapter four. But instead, the chapter presents a spectacular image of the throne of God. From the throne issue flashes of lightning and peals of thunders, around the throne are four living creatures chanting praises to God, and 24 elders fall down on a floor that is like a sea of glass and cast their golden crowns before the Lord. On the throne itself is one who is beyond description, because God cannot be described in mere words, except to say that God's appearance is like that of radiant jewels. And all the host of heaven join in a song, singing, "You are worthy, our Lord and God, to receive glory and honor and power." (Revelation 4:11)

This is a powerful image, and it would have communicated a particularly poignant message to the Christians in the first century, as they faced great pressure to offer worship to the emperor Domitian, who insisted on being worshiped and addressed as "our Lord and God." To disobey could cost one's life. It seemed at the time that all power was concentrated in Rome.

But the book of Revelation puts forth an inspiring image of the true throne and the real center of power in the universe. Significantly, all the host around God's throne ascribe *to God alone* the title that Domitian wanted! They say, "You are worthy, our Lord and God, to receive glory and honor and power!" (Revelation 4:11) The message to beleaguered Christians in the first century was clear: do not give in to worship the emperor; worship God alone, and trust in the Lord, because in spite of appearances, real power belongs to God, and God is on the throne.

The book of Revelation communicates the same message to the modern age! Christians today are often under pressure to compromise their faith, giving allegiance elsewhere; and it often seems that ungodly forces have the upper hand in this world. But the book of Revelation says: do not lose heart; give your loyalty only to God, and trust in the Lord, because God alone has true power—God is on the throne.

The vision in chapter five continues with a striking image of how God expresses power. The way in which God will use power was already indicated in chapter one, where, in a vision of Christ, a sword was depicted not in Christ's hand, as though Christ exercises a violent power, but issuing from his mouth. God's power, in short, is expressed through His *word*. A complementary image is found in the early part of chapter four, where it is said that a rainbow arches over the throne of God—a reminder of God's promise to Noah that God will not use power to obliterate the world, but will act in mercy. Now in chapter five, one can see yet more clearly how God acts.

In this chapter, God holds a sealed scroll. In apocalyptic writing, a scroll typically symbolizes the decrees of God. An angel calls out, asking, "Who is worthy to break open the seals?" At first it appears there is no one worthy, but then one of the elders says to John, "The Lion of Judah—namely Christ—is worthy." (Revelation 5:5)

In keeping with the flow of the vision, one now expects a lion to come roaring onto the stage. But suddenly, what John sees is *a lamb*, a lamb which looks as though it had been slain. (Revelation 5:6)

This is a dramatic picture of how God has expressed power in Christ. People in first-century Israel, when they thought of a Messiah, expected a lion—a figure who would burst forth with great power and devour their enemies. But instead of a lion, Christ came as the lamb—as one who lived in love and peace and who gave his life for others. Quite significantly, the vision in Revelation says that Christ is still the Lamb. Christ is pictured in the vision as a lamb with seven eyes and seven horns (Revelation 5:6). In apocalyptic writing, the number 7 represents completeness or the fullness of God, as noted above. Eyes represent insight; so seven eyes indicate that Christ has the fullness of divine insight. Horns in apocalyptic writing are a symbol for power, so seven horns indicate that Christ has the fullness of divine power. Yet it is all expressed in the form of a sacrificial lamb, which means that *the power of God takes the form of the lamb, in the self-giving love of Christ*.

All this says a great deal about how people should expect God to act. The image of the lamb says that God will express power not in brute force to destroy God's enemies, but in appealing love, to redeem those who are far from God. The Oxford Biblical scholar G. B. Caird summed it up well when he said that Christ as lamb "redefines omnipotence. Omnipotence is not to be understood as the power of unlimited coercion, but as the power of infinite persuasion, the invincible power of self-negating, self-sacrificing love."v

This understanding provides insight into the apparent contradiction that is inherent in the vision—namely, if God is on the throne of the universe, if God is in charge, why is it that evil still rages on earth? The answer is that God in grace refuses to simply crush evil with brute power. That is good news for all who are sinners—to realize that in spite of human imperfections, the Lord comes not as a lion ready to tear sinners to shreds but as a lamb offering forgiveness. And it is good news for a wayward world, that God's intention is not to destroy humanity but to renew it.

The vision gives a further message about how humanity is now called to live in the world. Human beings are called to follow the way of the lamb. The image of the victorious lamb says that true victory over evil will come not by force but by the transforming love of Christ. That is exactly the approach the early Christians took in the late first century and beyond. They did not attack the Roman Empire—*they converted it.*

Often people want to imagine that the book of Revelation declares that God will come with devastating wrath to destroy the sinners of the world. Yet these early visions in Revelation declare precisely the opposite—that Christ comes to transform the world with grace. The Christ of Revelation is the same Christ of the gospels—One who meets a wayward world with redeeming love.

In the meantime, there will continue to be evil in the world. This is the price of God's loving approach, which allows people to reject God's ways. Times therefore can get rough, and that will be apparent as the visions in Revelation continue to unfold. But when it seems that the world is out of control, and evil is running the show, it is good to remember the vision of John—that the one who sits upon the throne of the universe is the God of love. When people of faith take hold of that vision, they can join with the heavenly host in singing: "To him who sits upon the throne and to the lamb be blessing and honor and glory and might forever and ever!" (Revelation 5:13)

THE FOUR HORSEMEN
REVELATION CHAPTERS 6 AND 7

Then I saw the Lamb open one of the seven seals, and I heard one of the four living creatures call out, as with a voice of thunder, "Come!" I looked, and there was a white horse! Its rider had a bow; a crown was given to him, and he came out conquering and to conquer.

When he opened the second seal, I heard the second living creature call out, "Come!" And out came another horse, bright red; its rider was permitted to take peace from the earth, so that people would slaughter one another; and he was given a great sword. When he opened the third seal, I heard the third living creature call out, "Come!" I looked, and there was a black horse! Its rider held a pair of scales in his hand, and I heard what seemed to be a voice in the midst of the four living creatures saying, "A quart of wheat for a day's pay, and three quarts of barley for a day's pay, but do not damage the olive oil and the wine!" When he opened the fourth seal, I heard the voice of the fourth living creature call out, "Come!" I looked and there was a pale green horse! Its rider's name was Death, and Hades followed with him; they were given authority over a fourth of the earth, to kill with sword, famine, and pestilence, and by the wild animals of the earth.

When he opened the fifth seal, I saw under the altar the souls of those who had been slaughtered for the word of God and for the testimony they had given; they cried out with a loud voice, "Sovereign Lord, holy and true, how long will it be before you judge and avenge our blood on the inhabitants of the earth?" They were each given a white robe and told to rest a little longer, until the number would be complete both of their fellow servants and of their brothers and sisters, who were soon to be killed as they themselves had been killed. When he opened the sixth seal, I looked, and there came a great earthquake; the sun became black as sackcloth, the full moon became like blood, and the stars of the sky fell to the earth as the fig tree drops its winter fruit when shaken by a gale. The sky vanished like a scroll rolling itself up, and every mountain and island was removed from its place. Then the kings of the earth and the magnates and the generals and the rich and the powerful, and everyone, slave and free, hid in the caves and among the rocks of the mountains, calling to the mountains and rocks, "Fall on us and hide us from the face of the one seated on the throne and from the wrath of the Lamb; for the great day of their wrath has come, and who is able to stand?"

Revelation 6:1–17

After this I saw four angels standing at the four corners of the earth, holding back the four winds of the earth so that no wind could blow on earth or sea or against any tree. I saw another angel ascending from the rising of the sun, having the seal of the living God, and he called with a loud voice to the four angels who had been given power to damage earth and sea, saying, "Do not damage the earth or the sea or the trees, until we have marked the servants of our God with a seal on their foreheads." And I heard the number of those who were sealed, one hundred forty-four thousand, sealed out of every tribe of the people of Israel: After this I looked, and there was a great multitude that no one could count, from every nation, from all tribes and peoples and languages, standing before the throne and before the Lamb, robed in white, with palm branches in their hands. They cried out in a loud voice, saying, "Salvation belongs to our God who is seated on the throne, and to the Lamb!" And all the angels stood around the throne and around the elders and the four living creatures, and they fell on their faces before the throne and worshiped God, singing, "Amen! Blessing and glory and wisdom and thanksgiving and honor and power and might be to our God forever and ever! Amen."

Then one of the elders addressed me, saying, "Who are these, robed in white, and where have they come from?" I said to him, "Sir, you are the one that knows." Then he said to me, "These are they who have come out of the great ordeal; they have washed their robes and made them white in the blood of the Lamb. For this reason they are before the throne of God, and worship him day and night within his temple, and the one who is seated on the throne will shelter them. They will hunger no more, and thirst no more; the sun will not strike them, nor any scorching heat; for the Lamb at the center of the throne will be their shepherd, and he will guide them to springs of the water of life, and God will wipe away every tear from their eyes."

Revelation 7:1–4, 9–17

Revelation chapter six presents one of the most famous images of the book—the four horsemen. The four horsemen sweep across the earth, and they bring a whole series of catastrophes—war, famine, and death.

One of the ways that people have interpreted the four horsemen is to see them as cosmic figures who will come during the "end times" and who will usher in a period of great calamity. Jesus did say that things would get rough before His return. So a popular approach among end-times preachers has been to point at the many calamities in our world and then proclaim that all this trouble is precisely what the book of Revelation is predicting! The four horsemen are riding, one is told—the end times are upon us.

Some years ago, Richard DeHaan, who took over his father's Radio Bible Class and then became one of the early televangelists, produced a popular pamphlet along this line entitled "Warning: The Horsemen Are Coming." He said, "The mounting problems of overpopulation, food shortage, pollution, and political strife all seem to point toward the end of the age. And if it is drawing to a close, the time of the outpouring of God's wrath and judgment upon a wicked world is at hand."[vi]

Or consider the Italian commentator Joachim de Fiore. He put out a booklet in which he pointed out the rampant immorality in the world and the violence and crises that are afflicting the globe. He noted the visions in the book of Revelation and elsewhere and concluded that they are being fulfilled in the decay and disaster that are plaguing our earth. He finally said, "[The end of the age] will not take place in the days of your grandchildren or in the old age of your children, but in our own days, few and evil."[vii]

Joachim de Fiore wrote in the twelfth century. The fact is that for centuries people have been making exactly the same argument: they have pointed at the troubles in their age and have said, "Look at all this mayhem; it is proof that 'the horsemen are riding,' and the end is at hand." It is a common tendency to think that one's own time has gotten so bad that God must be about ready to bring down the curtain on world history. People seem to forget just how bad things were in previous times; and people seem to forget the words of Jesus, who said that when you see all kinds of troubles, do not be alarmed, because it is only the birthpangs of the kingdom of God. (Matthew 24:6–7)

To rightly understand the book of Revelation, it is essential to avoid speculation and to pay attention to what each image in the book was actually intended to say. The modern reader must begin by asking *what each image signified to the first-century audience to which the book was addressed.* With this approach, the real meaning of the four horsemen becomes clear.

The images in Revelation were familiar symbols for the first-century readers, because the pictures in Revelation draw on commonly known images found in the Old Testament or in the surrounding first-century culture. The image of the four horsemen alludes first of all to the book of Zechariah, where the prophet described an image of four chariots with red, black, white, and dappled gray horses. (Zechariah 6:1–8) There is a reason why there are *four.* It is because of the basic principle in apocalyptic writing that numbers have established symbolic meanings, and the number four represents the four directions of the earth. In Zechariah, this is made very clear when it is said that the four chariots "go forth to the four winds of heaven" (Zechariah 6:5) — north, south, east, and west. Chariots are a symbol of power, and so in Zechariah the chariots symbolize powers extending across the earth.

The four horsemen in Revelation will thus represent forces that stretch across the world. The significance of the colors is not elaborated in Zechariah, but the meaning of the four colors is much more developed in Revelation. The significance of the colors is to be found by looking at the meaning of each color in the ancient setting.

The first horseman appears on a white horse. In general in apocalyptic writing, white is a symbol for victory, but "victory" may or may not be a good thing, depending on what sort of power is achieving the victory! In a Hollywood western, the good guy rides on a white horse, but it is not so here. This vision is a prime example of the fact that it is only by looking at the first-century setting that one can rightly and fully understand these visions. This rider on a white horse carries a bow. In the first century, a horseman with a bow sitting on a white horse represented one thing—a Parthian warrior. The Parthians were a fierce, warlike people who ruled a vast empire that stretched 1,500 miles to the east of the Roman Empire. They were known for their brutality and their territory-grabbing, and their armies were unique in featuring mounted archers who preferred white horses. To a first-century reader, looking at an image of a mounted archer on a white horse would have engendered the same kind of feeling that a contemporary person would have when looking at an image of a goose-stepping soldier with a swastika on the arm. The image conveyed an unmistakable impression of brutal conquest.

What follows in the vision is what always follows human conquest. The red horse coming next clearly symbolizes bloodshed and the suffering of war, as the rider wields a sword and takes peace from the earth. Next comes the black horse—black symbolizes the lack of something—and the vision describes famine, as it speaks of a day's wage buying just a quart of wheat, which was one twelfth of what it would normally buy. Warfare and famine are finally followed by a pale horse. In the original Greek, the word describing this horse's color actually means greenish gray—the color of a corpse—and the name of the rider is death.

The vision of the four horsemen is thus a poignant image of four very negative forces that race across the earth—conquest, bloodshed, famine, and death. There is no reason to think of these horsemen as depictions of future realities. In the first century, Christians had first-hand experience with everything the four horsemen represented—they knew conquest, bloodshed, famine, and death. Modern people have a similar range of experience, for these evils are in the headlines every day! In this light, it is quite significant that in virtually every century from the first century until now, people have looked around themselves and have sensed that the four horsemen were riding in their own time. At the beginning of the book of Revelation, it was said that the visions would represent "what is (what is in the first century) and what is to come (what is to follow thereafter)." Here it is plain that the four horsemen represent the persistent devastations that plague the whole human race in every age—the conquest, bloodshed, famine, and death that have been racing across the world stage from Biblical days to the present.

In short, the four horsemen are not predictions of a distant future; they are depictions of ongoing evils. But from where do these evils come? Does God send these terrors upon the earth? It is important to observe that the vision never says that God sends the four horsemen. It says that each horseman was "permitted" to ride. (Revelation 6:4) The basic picture is that God allows these evils to go forth, but does not directly cause them. The real cause of such evil, from the Biblical perspective, is human sinfulness—human grasping after power, human greed, and human hatred.

But then a larger question arises, a question that is the central issue of Revelation chapter six. The question comes into focus when the fifth seal is opened to reveal the martyrs—those Christians who were tortured and killed because of their witness, which was happening with frequency during the early persecutions. The martyrs were victims of the evil depicted in the four horsemen; and they cry out, "How long, O Lord, must all this go on? When, O God, will you act with justice?" (Revelation 6:10)

Today people ask the same question. They see the four horsemen riding—they see terrible evils ripping across the globe—and they ask the central question, Where is God in the face of this evil? How long must terrorist attacks and racist prejudice and world hunger and all kinds of injustice go on? Will God ever act?

This was a critical question for Christians in the late first century. They believed in a good and loving God, but they saw horrible evils happening to good people, and they were asking, "Where is God?"

To this question, the book of Revelation gives an unequivocal answer: *God is in charge.* The only reason that evils are running through the world, says the vision, is because God for this time permits it, because God allows people the freedom to choose against God and to abuse power and to commit great sin. But God is not passive. In the vision, God actually limits what the four horsemen can do; and then, when the sixth seal is opened, it becomes clear that God will ultimately act in judgment against evil. The sixth seal portrays a giant earthquake and whole series of images that are drawn from the Old Testament prophets — the sun becoming black and the moon becoming like blood and the stars falling from the sky. Again, this is not meant to be understood literally. These are classic images of the wrath of God against sin, and the vision goes on to talk about sinners fleeing and mountains collapsing. What is clear from the vision is that God does and will act, and God will ultimately shatter every power of evil.

But what about those who are already victims of evil? The vision answers this concern in chapter seven with a tremendous portrait of 144,000 people who have been "sealed" by God. In the ancient world, a seal denoted ownership, and thus the vision portrays a host of people who *belong to God.*

Why are there 144,000? A classic misunderstanding of this passage is offered by Jehovah's Witnesses, who take the number literally and claim that it means there will be exactly 144,000 people in heaven, which means, it seems, that there is going to be some serious competition. Here is a prime example of why it is important to understand the way that apocalyptic writing uses numbers symbolically. Paying attention to the symbolic meanings will quickly reveal the significance of 144,000. The number 12, being the number of the tribes of Israel and the number of Jesus' disciples, signifies the people of God, while 1,000 represents completeness or *the whole number* of something. So 12 times 12 times 1,000 — 144,000 — represents *the whole number of the people of God*. Indeed right after talking about 144,000, John begins talking about "a great multitude that no one could count, standing before the throne and the Lamb." (Revelation 7:9) They have palm branches, signs of God's victory, and they are shouting praise, saying "Salvation belongs to our God." (Revelation 7:10) This is finally a simple and straightforward image which says that all who live in faith will be brought by God through the ordeals of life and will stand finally in joy before the throne of the Lord.

The message of the whole vision becomes clear. The forces of evil at times run roughshod over the world, and it may be difficult to make sense out of what is happening around us; but although it may seem that the world is being overrun with trouble, God is still in charge. As John Wesley, founder of the Methodist movement, put it: "The four horsemen, as with their first entrance in [Roman times], so with all their entrances in succeeding ages… are in all ages subject to Christ."[viii] Because God is in charge, people of faith can have confidence that God's victory will finally prevail. Evil will ultimately be judged and vanquished, and those who have faith in the Lord will be brought through every ordeal and brought at last into the eternal kingdom of God.

The four horsemen are riding in our time; but those who trust in Christ need not lose hope. They can know instead that their sure destiny is the promise expressed in the vision at the close of chapter seven: "They shall hunger no more, neither thirst any more; the sun shall not strike them, nor any scorching heat. For the lamb in the midst of the throne will be their shepherd, and he will guide them to springs of living water; and God will wipe away every tear from their eyes." (Revelation 7:16–17)

THE SEVENTH SEAL
REVELATION CHAPTERS 8 AND 9

When the Lamb opened the seventh seal, there was silence in heaven for about half an hour. And I saw the seven angels who stand before God, and seven trumpets were given to them. Another angel with a golden censer came and stood at the altar; he was given a great quantity of incense to offer with the prayers of all the saints on the golden altar that is before the throne. And the smoke of the incense, with the prayers of the saints, rose before God from the hand of the angel. Then the angel took the censer and filled it with fire from the altar and threw it on the earth; and there were peals of thunder, rumblings, flashes of lightning, and an earthquake. Now the seven angels who had the seven trumpets made ready to blow them.

The first angel blew his trumpet, and there came hail and fire, mixed with blood, and they were hurled to the earth; and a third of the earth was burned up, and a third of the trees were burned up, and all green grass was burned up. The second angel blew his trumpet, and something like a great mountain, burning with fire, was thrown into the sea. A third of the sea became blood, a third of the living creatures in the sea died, and a third of the ships were destroyed. The third angel blew his trumpet, and a great star fell from heaven, blazing like a torch, and it fell on a third of the rivers and on the springs of water. The name of the star is Wormwood. A third of the waters became wormwood, and many died from the water, because it was made bitter. The fourth angel blew his trumpet, and a third of the sun was struck, and a third of the moon, and a third of the stars, so that a third of their light was darkened; a third of the day was kept from shining, and likewise the night. Then I looked, and I heard an eagle crying with a loud voice as it flew in midheaven, "Woe, woe, woe to the inhabitants of the earth, at the blasts of the other trumpets that the three angels are about to blow!"

Revelation 8:1–13

And the fifth angel blew his trumpet, and I saw a star that had fallen from heaven to earth, and he was given the key to the shaft of the bottomless pit; he opened the shaft of the bottomless pit, and from the shaft rose smoke like the smoke of a great furnace, and the sun and the air were darkened with the smoke from the shaft. Then from the smoke came locusts on the earth, and they were given authority like the authority of scorpions of the earth. They were told not to damage the grass of the earth or any green growth or any tree, but only those people who do not have the seal of God on their foreheads. They were allowed to torture them for five months, but not to kill them, and their torture was like the torture of a scorpion when it stings someone. And in those days people will seek death but will not find it; they will long to die, but death will flee from them. In appearance the locusts were like horses equipped for battle. On their heads were what looked like crowns of gold; their faces were like human faces, their hair like women's hair, and their teeth like lions' teeth; they had scales like iron breastplates, and the noise of their wings was like the noise of many chariots with horses rushing into battle. They have tails like scorpions, with stingers, and in their tails is their power to harm people for five months.

Revelation 9:1–10

I n 1957, the Swedish film director Ingmar Bergman produced a film that received much critical acclaim entitled *The Seventh Seal.* The film was unrelentingly grim and depressing, which means it had an appropriate title, because out of the entire book of Revelation, the section about the seventh seal is the gloomiest.

In ancient times, when an important missive was sent, it was closed up with a seal (envelopes having not yet been invented). Document seals were made out of wax, generally with an impression indicating the identity of the sender. The recipient opened the seal to receive the message. This is the image governing the "seven seals" of the book of Revelation; the opening of each seal reveals each successive message.

The sequence began in chapter five with the image of a scroll "sealed with seven seals" (Revelation 5:1) and the question, "Who is worthy to break open the seals?" (Revelation 5:2). Not just anyone was permitted to open an important letter! The vision proceeds with the declaration that Christ (the Lamb) is the one who is worthy (Revelation 5:5), and through the opening of the seals it is the Lamb who opens each one. The clear picture is that Christ is the one who reveals the truths of God!

The actual opening of the seals began in chapter six. The first four seals revealed the four horsemen, who brought conquest, bloodshed, famine, and death across the earth. The fifth seal revealed the vision of the martyrs who were suffering under persecution. The sixth seal revealed the great earthquake that brought terror upon sinners, but which was followed by a glorious vision of the martyrs having been brought through persecution into the joy of heaven. Throughout the first six seals, there is a message that evil and trouble are racing across the earth, and the faithful may suffer, but God is at work with judgment and saving power, and the faithful will finally be brought through every ordeal to share in the victory of God's Kingdom.

Chapter eight begins with the opening of the seventh seal. One might expect that this seal will be the conclusion of things. Has the reader not already seen enough trouble? But the opening of the seventh seal initiates an entirely new cycle—the seven trumpets. Trumpets in the ancient world were used to announce something important; and in this sequence each trumpet announces a successive vision, and each vision reveals more trouble. This is a portrayal of our human condition that resonates through the ages. Just when it seems that one set of troubles is past, a new round of trouble emerges!

The first trumpet signals hail and fire and blood falling on the earth. The second trumpet signals a flaming mountain being thrown into the sea, an image that would have resonated with first-century readers in light of the then-recent explosion of Mt. Vesuvius at Pompeii. The third trumpet signals a star falling from heaven called Wormwood, the name of a common plant with a very bitter juice which was a Biblical symbol of bitterness, and the star poisons water on earth. The fourth trumpet causes a third of the sun and stars and moon to be darkened, again an Old Testament symbol of doom, and the fifth trumpet sets off a plague of fiendish locusts, which emerge out of a shaft of a bottomless pit to torment humanity. Finally, the sixth trumpet sends forth a kind of monster cavalry.

The seventh trumpet will not arrive until chapter 11. One might expect that this last trumpet would be the welcome conclusion to all these woes; but in fact the seventh trumpet will be followed by a whole new series—the seven bowls of wrath.

Many people avoid the book of Revelation for this very reason. It is so full of gloom and doom! It seems to many people that the whole tone of the book conflicts with the tone of the rest of the New Testament. Where is the upbeat message of love and promise that is the dominant theme elsewhere? What is one to do with the dark imagery in the book of Revelation?

The book of Revelation is full of dark imagery because it was written during exceptionally dark times—the beginning of the great persecution of Christians under the Roman emperors. One possible response to dark times is to try to "look at the bright side." A teenage boy once announced to his father, "Good news, Dad, the car insurance you bought is finally going to pay off." There can certainly be a benefit sometimes to try to look at the bright side; but in the midst of truly rough times, a forced attempt at cheerfulness simply does not take reality seriously. As one verse in the book of Proverbs puts it: "To a person with a heavy heart, singing happy songs is like vinegar in a wound." (Proverbs 25:20)

The book of Revelation takes the dark times seriously. It hits the depths of human evil and tragedy head-on. Many of the images in Revelation are graphic portrayals of evil and calamity. The images are not meant to be understood literally. They are more like surrealistic paintings which are meant to figuratively convey something of the twisted nature of the world. A prime example of this can be found within the trumpet sequence in the vision of the locusts.

The vision of the locusts, in chapter nine, is one of the most horrifying visions in the entire book of Revelation. These creatures come swarming out of the bowels of the earth; they have fangs like lions and iron-like scales and thundering wings and tails that sting like a scorpion. They swoop down on people and cause them excruciating pain. Some end-times interpreters have wanted to see these locusts as actual demonic entities that God will send on a sinful world in the last days. But such an understanding would make God vicious—a clear contradiction of the rest of the New Testament! The mistake that people make in such cases is to try to read the book of Revelation too literally. As Biblical scholars will ofttimes suggest, the book of Revelation does not mean what it says (in literal terms). *It means what it means*—its visions are pictures which are intended to be viewed for their symbolic meaning.

In the vision of the locusts, John the author of Revelation presents us with a composite picture of all the things that caused

first-century people real fear. Locusts themselves were the ultimate plague and were greatly feared for their destructive power.
These locusts are pictured further with fangs like lions—lions
were still a danger in various areas and were used by Romans
as an instrument of persecution; Tertullian, writing a century
after the book of Revelation, spoke of Christians being thrown
to the lions.[ix] The scales like iron would have called to mind the
armor of soldiers, who again in Roman times were a great threat
to Christians and Jews, and the scorpion sting was one of the
dangerous poisons that could be encountered in the semi-arid
regions around the Mediterranean. In short, the vision takes classic sources of terror—all those things that were actually causing
people real fear—and rolls them all together into one. The locusts
are a gripping symbol of everything in the world that would cause
people fear and pain.

In this context, it is important to note that the locusts in the
vision are not actually sent from God. They emerge from a pit,
and they are "allowed" (Revelation 9:5) by God to fly against humanity. Moreover, the extent of what they can do is limited by
God—they are not allowed to kill anyone, and their time period
is limited. All this is a symbolic way of saying that God does not
send terror and pain; and even as God may allow trouble to happen, God works to limit the effect of calamities. But what then is
the actual source of all the terror and pain in the world?

Significantly, the locusts are said to have *human faces* (Revelation 9:7)—which is a striking, symbolic way of saying that evil
very often has a human face, a human origin. The book of Revelation, along with the Bible as a whole, consistently proclaims that
the ultimate cause of the twisted nature of the world is human
sinfulness.

But what then is God's action in all this? The most important
part of the vision of the locusts is the statement that the locusts
will not attack those who have the seal of God upon their forehead
(Revelation 9:4). In ancient times, a seal was used to indicate pos-
session. In addition to the wax seals on documents, showing the
identity of the sender, there were all sorts of other seals made out

of clay or other materials, which indicated ownership or authority over something. A vintner, for example, would put a seal on his jars of wine to show that they came from his vineyard. To say that people have the seal of God upon them is to say that *they belong to God;* they are under the power and protection of the Lord.

The vision finally declares that those who belong to God will be under God's protection against the power of evil. Does this mean that if you believe in God, nothing bad can happen to you? That could scarcely have been John's message, since he himself was in prison, and his fellow Christians were being tortured and killed for their faith at the time of his writing the book of Revelation. John was well aware that people of faith can encounter dark times; he depicts this reality continually! But throughout the book of Revelation there is a consistent theme that even if the faithful are in the midst of great trial and distress, they can trust in God that *evil will not overwhelm the faithful,* but God will be present with a protecting power to sustain God's people through evil and even finally through death. This was Revelation's promise to Christians who were encountering truly rough times.

But what does God finally do about evil itself? It is this question that most of the images in these chapters are answering, because the visions have to do with God's judgment against evil. It is common for end-times predictors to want to take these visions literally and suggest that they are predictions of actual acts of judgment on humanity's evil, with the further suggestion that these predictions are starting to unfold right now. Several years ago, Jack Van Impe, an American televangelist, proclaimed that the vision of the third trumpet—with a toxic star named Wormwood falling from heaven (Revelation 8:10–11)—was fulfilled in the Chernobyl nuclear accident, because in the Ukrainian language the name "Wormwood" is rendered "Chernobyl." If you look far enough and inventively enough, you can find "fulfillments" of the images of Revelation everywhere!

To rightly understand the visions, it is essential to pay attention to the actual intended references of the images. A great deal of the imagery in Revelation is drawn straight out of the Old Testament;

and in the trumpet sequence, every image has an Old Testament backdrop, where the images serve as classic symbols for God's wrath being expressed against the wicked. These images are not predictions of future events; they are depictions of the way in which God's wrath *throughout time* moves against evil.

What then are Christians to think about the whole idea of God's wrath? There are two ways in which Christians today commonly react to the theme of God's wrath, especially as it comes forth in the book of Revelation. One approach is to welcome the notion of God's wrath with *schadenfreude,* longing for disaster to befall the wicked. Many end-times preachers find a kind of glee in pronouncing the torments of Revelation that they expect and hope will soon come crashing upon the sinners of the world.

The other common approach is to avoid the theme of God's wrath altogether. With this approach, people simply ignore the related imagery in Revelation, and recast God as a more docile figure. The late Biblical scholar Harrell F. Beck once suggested that the God of the popular imagination is a "great mush God," who does not stand for much, and who never would presume to call anyone to account. The book of Revelation offers a valuable corrective to this tendency to turn God into mush, for the book makes plain that while God exercises enormous patience, God is angered at evil, and God will ultimately act in judgment against evil.

The book of Revelation thus presses Christians to come to terms with the wrath of God. Yet this wrath must not be seen as a contradiction of God's love. God's wrath is God's righteous anger, and it is understood in the Bible as an aspect of God's love. God is like a parent who loves a child and who therefore will become angry when a child does wrong and may exercise punishment in order to correct the child. At the end of chapter nine there is a lament that in spite of all the trumpets people did not repent (Revelation 9:20–21). The aim of God always is to move humanity to *repent*—to turn to God and to find God's redeeming love and mercy.

Christians appropriately respond to Revelation's message of wrath not by yearning for punishment on unbelievers but by joining with God in this movement of seeking to draw the world toward repentance. At the same time, the message of God's wrath, which is signaled in the trumpets, declares finally that *evil will be defeated.* Evil will be continually defeated through history by the working of God, and will be ultimately defeated at the end of time. Evil may rage, but God's righteousness will finally triumph. Believers are thus encouraged never to despair in the face of evil but to persevere in faith.

The book of Revelation pulls no punches when it comes to dealing with the dark side of life. In gripping terms, the imagery of the book portrays the terrors and pains of this world, and the sin and brokenness of human life. In the face of truly dark times, the book of Revelation does not offer a meager counsel to try to look at the bright side. Instead, the book calls us to look to God, for it is God who out of human darkness will create a bright future. This is where the book of Revelation is moving—through dark and terrifying visions toward a vision at the end of the book that is the brightest and most glorious vision in the Bible of God's destiny for humanity. The overarching message of the book is that it is God who can bring human beings through the dark times into a bright future. In the end, there is a bright side—in the future that God will create for all who would put their trust in the Lord.

WITNESSES FOR GOD
REVELATION CHAPTERS 10 AND 11

Then the voice that I had heard from heaven spoke to me again, saying, "Go, take the scroll that is open in the hand of the angel who is standing on the sea and on the land." So I went to the angel and told him to give me the little scroll; and he said to me, "Take it, and eat; it will be bitter to your stomach, but sweet as honey in your mouth." So I took the little scroll from the hand of the angel and ate it; it was sweet as honey in my mouth, but when I had eaten it, my stomach was made bitter. Then they said to me, "You must prophesy again about many peoples and nations and languages and kings."

Revelation 10:8–11

Then I was given a measuring rod like a staff, and I was told, "Come and measure the temple of God and the altar and those who worship there, but do not measure the court outside the temple; leave that out, for it is given over to the nations, and they will trample over the holy city for forty-two months.

And I will grant my two witnesses authority to prophesy for one thousand two hundred sixty days, wearing sackcloth." These are the two olive trees and the two lampstands that stand before the Lord of the earth. And if anyone wants to harm them, fire pours from their mouth and consumes their foes; anyone who wants to harm them must be killed in this manner. They have authority to shut the sky, so that no rain may fall during the days of their prophesying, and they have authority over the waters to turn them into blood, and to strike the earth with every kind of plague, as often as they desire. When they have finished their testimony, the beast that comes up from the bottomless pit will make war on them and conquer them and kill them, and their dead bodies will lie in the street of the great city that is prophetically called Sodom and Egypt, where also their Lord was crucified. For three and a half days members of the peoples and tribes and languages and nations will gaze at their dead bodies and refuse to let them be placed in a tomb; and the inhabitants of the earth will gloat over them and celebrate and exchange presents, because these two prophets had been a torment to the inhabitants of the earth. But after the three and a half days, the breath of life from God entered them, and they stood on their feet, and those who saw them were terrified. Then they heard a loud voice from heaven saying to them, "Come up here!" And they went up to heaven in a cloud while their enemies watched them. At that moment there was a great earthquake, and a tenth of the city fell; seven thousand people were killed in the earthquake, and the rest were terrified and gave glory to the God of heaven.

The second woe has passed. The third woe is coming very soon. Then the seventh angel blew his trumpet, and there were loud voices in heaven, saying, "The kingdom of the world has become the kingdom of our Lord and of his Messiah, and he will reign forever and ever."

Revelation 11:1–15

The picture in chapter 11 of the two witnesses is one of the strangest images in the entire book of Revelation—which says a great deal, since the book of Revelation has its share of bizarre images! Chapter 11 presents the vision of two witnesses, who will prophesy to the world for 1,260 days, that is, three and a half years. The witnesses are pictured figuratively as two olive trees or two lampstands. If anyone tries to harm these two witnesses, fire will come out of the mouths of the witnesses and obliterate them. The witnesses are portrayed as having other amazing powers—the power to shut the sky and prevent it from raining, or the power to turn rivers into blood or smite the earth with plagues.

Finally, however, a beast will ascend from the bottomless pit, will make war upon the two witnesses and kill them, after which their bodies will lie for three and a half days in Jerusalem, causing people to rejoice and exchange presents. But then God will resurrect the witnesses, instilling great fear in their adversaries, and will raise the witnesses up to heaven, after which an earthquake will devastate the city.

What is the contemporary reader to make of this? Who are the two witnesses, and what does the beast stand for, and what is the meaning of these time frames of three and a half years or days? It seems one could speculate endlessly about the meaning of this passage and come up with all kinds of interpretations.

This is precisely what has happened throughout the history of the church. In 1881 in Russia, Claas Epp, who was a leader of a Mennonite sect, declared that he was one of the two witnesses, that he was commissioned to proclaim the end of the world, and that he would soon meet Elijah in the sky. He announced that

Christ would return on March 8, 1889. God had revealed this date, Epp explained, in part by means of an old wall clock in which the hands pointed to 8 and 9. 1889 passed, however, quite uneventfully, after which Epp declared that God had revealed to him in the vision that the clock leaned slightly, and that when read correctly it would read 91. The new date of 1891 also turned out to be bogus, but that did not stop Epp! He declared himself to be a son of Christ and adopted a new baptismal formula of Father, Sons, and Holy Spirit.

It has always been possible to make wild speculations and claims based on the book of Revelation, and people who have wanted to advance themselves have been particularly inclined to do this. Yet, in fact, there is no need to speculate about the meaning of these images, and there is no need to be led astray by the claims of would-be prophets, because the keys to interpreting the images in Revelation are readily at hand. They are supplied in the Bible itself.

Of the 404 verses in the book of Revelation, 278 contain some sort of allusion to the Old Testament. Here is an example of why it is so important to understand the Old Testament in order to properly understand the New. The images in Revelation are rooted in and to a large extent draw their meaning from the Old Testament. In order to understand the book of Revelation, one does not need to look at old wall clocks or listen to wild claims; one needs to look in the pages of the Bible, for there the meanings of many images in Revelation are clearly established.

The image of the two olive trees (or two witnesses) comes from the book of Zechariah (chapter 4), where the two trees stand for King Zerubbabel and the high priest Jeshua (or Joshua)—two men of faith who were to proclaim the truth of God to the newly reestablished kingdom of Judah after the exile in the sixth century BC. But lest the witnesses be too specifically identified with Zerubbabel and Jeshua, the image in Revelation goes on to call to mind two additional persons of faith out of the Old Testament. It is said of the two witnesses that they will have the power to turn rivers into blood and to shut up the sky and keep it from raining.

It was Moses who turned rivers to blood in Egypt, and it was Elijah who was given the power to prevent rain. Once again the vision portrays two persons, Moses and Elijah, who put their lives on the line to bear witness to the kingdom of God.

The two olive trees thus call to mind people of faith out of the Old Testament who were witnesses for God in difficult times. One could perhaps imagine on this basis that the olive trees represent two future individuals who will come one day and be like those Old Testament personages. Then one might have to take seriously the claims of people like Claas Epp! But John gives a further indication as to the meaning of the two olive trees when he says that the two witnesses or two olive trees are also two lampstands. This refers the reader back to the beginning of the book of Revelation, where lampstands represent churches or communities of Christians. The image thus becomes clear: the witnesses—the lampstands, the olive trees—represent all those in the churches who in the tradition of Moses and Elijah and Zerubbabel and Jeshua *bear witness for their faith* to the world.

Why are there two witnesses in the vision? This part of the vision is again based on the Old Testament, which specifies that whenever there is testimony to be given in a court of law, there must be at least two witnesses to corroborate the truth (see Deuteronomy 19:15). The implication is that there is a need for *multiple witnesses* for the gospel.

The import of the vision becomes clear when it is held against the backdrop of the first-century church, when Christians were facing pressure to renounce their faith and possible martyrdom. The vision strongly encourages Christians in the various congregations to continue to faithfully bear witness for the gospel. Just as Zerubbabel and Jeshua and Moses and Elijah had faithfully borne witness for God in the face of severe opposition, so now the early Christians were to speak courageously for God, confident that God would sustain them.

Verse five speaks of fire pouring forth from the mouths of the witnesses to slay their enemies. This again is a direct allusion to the Old Testament, to a Messianic passage in the prophet Isaiah, where Isaiah says, "With the breath of his mouth he will slay the wicked" (Isaiah 11:4). This is similar in nature to the earlier image in Revelation that depicts the sword of Christ coming forth from *his mouth.* Christians are thus called to defeat their enemies not with violence but by proclaiming the truth of God! The image of fire indicates further that God would empower their speech, since fire is a Biblical symbol of the presence and empowerment of God.

The situation of first-century Christians continues to be described as the vision unfolds. The vision speaks of a terrible beast who would arise and fight against the witnesses and kill them. The image of the beast is found originally in the Old Testament in the book of Daniel, where it has a clearly defined meaning. In Daniel, beasts represent worldly empires. The beast in Revelation chapter 11 would thus quite plainly represent the Roman Empire, which was fighting against the Christians and killing them. It is notable that the vision goes on to describe people rejoicing at the death of the witnesses. This reflects precisely the situation in the Roman Empire, where people who hated the Christians actually did rejoice upon the slaughter of Christian martyrs. The time frame of three and a half years is also an allusion to the book of Daniel, where a time frame of three and a half years is symbolic for a time of trouble.

The vision, however, does not end with the death of the witnesses. They are resurrected and taken to heaven. The world is shaken up by the whole experience—symbolized in the earthquake—and many people, it seems, are positively affected in the end, because the vision of the witnesses concludes with most people giving glory to God.

This vision brought a clear message in symbolic terms to the early Christian readers of the book. It called them to faithfully bear witness to the gospel, even though they would encounter frightening opposition in the Roman Empire. The vision was thus a continuation of the theme in chapter 10, where John was instructed to eat a scroll that contained the word of God; the scroll tasted sweet, a reference to the goodness of the gospel message, but it was then bitter to his stomach, a reference to the bitter consequences that he and others would face when they proclaimed the word of God. (Revelation 10:10) Nevertheless, the vision in chapter 11 assured Christians that their witness for God would ultimately have a positive effect, and that many people would finally respond in faith; and the vision assured them that they themselves would receive finally the reward of heaven.

What the vision proclaimed proved exactly true. Early Christians met frightening opposition, and many were put to death for their witness; but their witness had a tremendous impact, and ultimately the majority of people in the entire Roman Empire came to faith in Christ.

What then is the message of this vision for today? The vision applies to the present time, not because it is a prediction of future events, but because it is a model of God's call to the faithful in every age. The vision summons contemporary Christians to bear witness for the gospel, even if it means suffering negative consequences.

Consider one "modern-day" example in which the vision in chapter 11 became reality again. In the 1960's, Martin Luther King Jr. became a witness for God's truth. His message challenged the powers of his day and was not well received. The beast—in this case, the beast of racism—rose from the pit, fought against King, and finally killed him. That, however, was not the end of the story. The nation was shaken up by the whole experience, and in the end, America changed for the better; and King himself has surely inherited the promise of heaven.

Like many of the visions in Revelation, the vision of the witnesses describes an ongoing reality. New Testament professor James Efird put it this way: "Any time demonic evil takes control and persecutes the people of God and causes great hardship on earth, then the beast has come alive again and must be resisted by the witness of the faithful."[x] Christians are called in every age to speak out against wrong and to bear witness for the truth and love and righteousness of God.

The chapter concludes with the sounding of the seventh trumpet, which proclaims the victory of the kingdom of God. It is a very appropriate conclusion to this section on the witnesses, because it declares that the witness for God's truth ultimately will culminate in victory.

In a world full of chaos and evil, it may often seem that those who would stand for goodness and truth are on the losing side. This surely is how things appeared to early Christians. They were up against apparently hopeless odds and were losing ground. The Roman Empire, thoroughly pagan, was intent on stomping out their little movement entirely.

But the vision in Revelation declares that those who serve Christ are in fact on the winning side, because no matter how fierce and beastly the opposition may seem, Christ will finally win the victory. The vision calls the faithful to keep on in faith, to bear witness for Christ today, and to know that they will one day join in that heavenly chorus, which after the trumpet call is heard singing, "The kingdom of this world has become the kingdom of our Lord, and he will reign forever and ever." (Revelation 11:15)

THE VISION OF THE BEASTS
REVELATION CHAPTERS 12 AND 13

A great portent appeared in heaven: a woman clothed with the sun, with the moon under her feet, and on her head a crown of twelve stars. She was pregnant and was crying out in birthpangs, in the agony of giving birth. Then another portent appeared in heaven: a great red dragon, with seven heads and ten horns, and seven diadems on his heads. His tail swept down a third of the stars of heaven and threw them to the earth. Then the dragon stood before the woman who was about to bear a child, so that he might devour her child as soon as it was born. And she gave birth to a son, a male child, who is to rule all the nations with a rod of iron. But her child was snatched away and taken to God and to his throne; and the woman fled into the wilderness, where she has a place prepared by God, so that there she can be nourished for one thousand two hundred sixty days. And war broke out in heaven; Michael and his angels fought against the dragon. The dragon and his angels fought back, but they were defeated, and there was no longer any place for them in heaven. The great dragon was thrown down, that ancient serpent, who is called the Devil and Satan, the deceiver of the whole world—he was thrown down to the earth, and his angels were thrown down with him. So when the dragon saw that he had been thrown down to the earth, he pursued the woman who had given birth to the male child. But the woman was given the two wings of the great eagle, so that she could fly from the serpent into the wilderness, to her place where she is nourished for a time, and times, and half a time. Then from his mouth the serpent poured water like a river after the woman, to sweep her away with the flood. But the earth came to the help of the woman; it opened its mouth and swallowed the river that the dragon had poured from his mouth. Then the dragon was angry with the woman, and went off to make war on the rest of her children, those who keep the commandments of God and hold the testimony of Jesus.

Revelation 12:1–9, 13–17

And I saw a beast rising out of the sea having ten horns and seven heads; and on its horns were ten diadems, and on its heads were blasphemous names. And the beast that I saw was like a leopard, its feet were like a bear's, and its mouth was like a lion's mouth. And the dragon gave it his power and his throne and great authority. One of its heads seemed to have received a death-blow, but its mortal wound had been healed. In amazement the whole earth followed the beast. They worshiped the dragon, for he had given his authority to the beast, and they worshiped the beast, saying, "Who is like the beast, and who can fight against it?" The beast was given a mouth uttering haughty and blasphemous words, and it was allowed to exercise authority for forty-two months. It opened its mouth to utter blasphemies against God, blaspheming his name and his dwelling, that is, those who dwell in heaven. Also it was allowed to make war on the saints and to conquer them. It was given authority over every tribe and people and language and nation, and all the inhabitants of the earth will worship it, everyone whose name has not been written from the foundation of the world in the book of life of the Lamb that was slaughtered. Let anyone who has an ear listen: If you are to be taken captive, into captivity you go; if you kill with the sword, with the sword you must be killed. Here is a call for the endurance and faith of the saints.

Then I saw another beast that rose out of the earth; it had two horns like a lamb and it spoke like a dragon. It exercises all the authority of the first beast on its behalf, and it makes the earth and its inhabitants worship the first beast, whose mortal wound had been healed. It performs great signs, even making fire come down from heaven to earth in the sight of all; and by the signs that it is allowed to perform on behalf of the beast, it deceives the inhabitants of earth, telling them to make an image for the beast that had been wounded by the sword and yet lived; and it was allowed to give breath to the image of the beast so that the image of the beast could even speak and cause those who would not worship the image of the beast to be killed. Also it causes all, both small and great, both rich and poor, both free and slave, to be marked on the right hand or the forehead, so that no one can buy or sell who does not have the mark, that is, the name of the beast or the number of its name. This calls for wisdom: let anyone with understanding calculate the number of the beast, for it is the number of a person. Its number is six hundred sixty-six.

Revelation 13:1–18

Chapters 12 and 13 of the book of Revelation contain some of the most memorable images in the book, as they present the vision of the beasts. There are three beasts—first a dragon, then a beast with seven heads and ten horns, and then a beast with horns like a lamb but which spoke like a dragon. The beasts in their full description may strike modern readers as thoroughly bizarre, but to the original readers of the book in the first century, these images were not bizarre at all; they were obvious and perfectly clear in their meaning.

Imagine if, two thousand years from now, people found some newspapers from the twenty-first century and noticed in them some frequent cartoons that depicted a donkey and an elephant. What strange images these would seem to be! Imagine how people could speculate about what they might mean. Of course, if they wanted to understand what our newspapers were really saying, they would simply need to find out what the donkey and the elephant actually signified for us, and they would discover that these images are in fact quite simple.

The same is true for the symbols in Revelation. One of the biggest mistakes modern interpreters have made is that they have speculated about the images in Revelation. End-times predictors have been particularly inclined to do this. Some years ago, there was a widespread theory that the ten horns of the beast represented the ten nations of the European Common Market. It sounded quite convincing to many people at the time. Then the Common Market (now the EU) added more countries, so the theory started to fall apart; but the real problem with end-times predictors is that they simply have not paid attention to what the original writer of the book actually intended to say with these symbols.

When we look at what the symbols meant for the people in the first century, to whom the book was originally addressed, the meaning of each symbol becomes plain. The dragon in chapter 12 that pursues a woman and her child is openly identified in the chapter as Satan. The male child, who would rule the nations and who was caught up to God's throne, is obviously Jesus. The woman who gives birth to the child is not specifically Mary but the whole people of God. This is clear from the statement that she wears a crown with twelve stars — the number twelve being a symbol for the people of God — and it is clear from the reference at the end of the chapter, which says that the dragon would make war on the rest of the woman's offspring, the rest of her offspring being "those who keep the commandments of God and bear testimony to Jesus." (Revelation 12:17)

The basic image is that the dragon, Satan, pursues the people of God, or the church, symbolized by the woman. But the power of the dragon is broken by the Lord. This is symbolized in the middle of chapter 12 by a scene of warfare in heaven where the dragon is defeated; and while the dragon thereafter continues to pursue God's people, the point is that Christ has been victorious over evil, and the woman in the end escapes destruction. The aims of the dragon are foiled! The whole image thus speaks of a time of trial and persecution for the people of God — exactly what Christians in the first century were experiencing — but it promises that God's people will ultimately be protected from evil.

This is followed in chapter 13 by the image of a beast rising out of the sea. This beast has sometimes been identified as the "Antichrist." During the history of the church, a notion developed that a figure would emerge who would be antithetical to Christ — the Antichrist — and who would seek to usurp the authority of God on earth. Note, however, that the word "antichrist" never appears in the book of Revelation! In fact, the word never appears in the entire Bible except for a couple of minor references in two of the letters of John. In those letters, however, it is said that there are *many* "antichrists." (I John 2:18) An antichrist is defined in those Biblical letters simply as anyone who denies Christ and acts against Christ (see II John 1:7). The word is that there will be many such people.

Through the history of the church, however, an idea emerged that while the Bible talks about many antichrists, there might appear one day *the Antichrist:* a figure of total opposition to Christ who would bring the world into great final ruin. This idea of an ultimate Antichrist became increasingly popular in the Middle Ages; and people since then have had a field day identifying particular historical figures as the Antichrist! In the early Middle Ages, some people thought the Muslim Sultan Saladin was the Antichrist. Later, Napoleon was identified as the Antichrist, and in the twentieth century, Hitler, Stalin, and Mussolini were all given the designation. During the Protestant Reformation, Martin Luther said that the Pope qualified as the Antichrist. Today, the concept of the Antichrist has become extremely popular among end-times predictors, who often claim that the Antichrist is coming soon or is perhaps in the world already. The Antichrist is almost always assumed to be pictured in the beast in Revelation chapter 13.

To rightly understand that image of the beast, however, one must pay attention to its original, intended meaning! To the first-century readers of the book of Revelation, the meaning of the beast was obvious—as obvious as a donkey or an elephant in the political pages of the newspaper would be for people today. The image is taken directly from another Biblical book, the book of Daniel, where beasts are used to represent empires. Four different beasts are described in Daniel, each representing a different empire. In the book of Revelation, the beast in chapter 13 has characteristics of all four of Daniel's beasts. The early readers of the book would thus have understood the beast to be a representation of a worldly empire which would incorporate the characteristics of and perhaps the territory of Daniel's beasts. There was one empire in the first century which quite clearly met this description—the Roman Empire. Further details are supplied in Revelation which make this meaning of the beast absolutely clear.

It is said that the beast has seven heads. Later, in chapter 17, this beast will appear again, and it is stated that the seven heads represent seven kings (Revelation 17:10). Significantly, there were seven emperors in Rome between the time of Jesus and the time of the writing of the book of Revelation. Chapter 17 also says that the seven heads also represent the seven hills upon which the city connected with the beast is seated (Revelation 17:9). Everybody in the Roman Empire knew that Rome was the city on seven hills. When early Christians saw this beast described, they immediately understood that it symbolized the Roman Empire in all its beastly power.

A further interesting feature of the beast is that one of its heads — or kings — is said to have a mortal wound that had been healed. This would have been quickly understood at the time as a reference to the Emperor Nero. Nero had committed suicide, but there were rumors at the time that he actually was alive in the East and preparing a return.

Perhaps the most intriguing characteristic of the beast is the one mentioned at the very end of chapter 13, where it is said that the beast has a number, the number of 666. Once again, there has been tremendous speculation about the meaning of this number, along with the associated reference to "the mark of the beast." End-times predictors have often claimed that the mark of the beast is some sort of sinister number that evil opponents of God are going to use to control the world in the last days. It has been suggested that the universal product code (the bar code on packages at the store) has the number 666 worked into it and is the mark of the beast. There have been long-running conspiracy theories that there is a giant computer in Belgium known as the Beast that has a number which is to be assigned to everybody, or that there is a plot by governments to surgically implant an identifying number into everyone, and that this sinister design to control humanity will be the mark of the beast.

Once again, it is crucial to ask what the number 666 actually meant for the original intended readers of the book, for then it becomes apparent that this is not a mysterious or sinister number at all; its meaning was obvious. The number six had a symbolic meaning—it represented human beings, since God created human beings on the sixth day. In the combination 666, however, it appears in a trinity of three. The number three is supposed to represent God—Father, Son, and Holy Spirit. Thus to early Christian readers, familiar with number symbolism, the human number 6 posing as a trinity—666—would have suggested a human being trying to be like God. There was also a sense in which the number 6 could represent incompleteness or evil—being one less that the perfect number of 7—so 666 could suggest a trinity of evil, or evil masquerading as divine.

In addition to these general symbolic references, the number 666 also had a very specific meaning. In the first century, every letter of the alphabet had a numerical value. This meant that every name had a corresponding number. To get the number of a person's name, one simply added up the numerical values of each of the letters in the name. It was a widespread practice to use numbers for people's names in this fashion, especially to make a coy reference. For example, on the walls of Pompeii there is a line of graffiti which says, "I love the girl whose name is 545."

Whose name adds up to 666? Scholars have tried all kinds of first-century names, and they have found one very likely name that adds up to 666. It is the name of Caesar Nero. Caesar Nero adds up to 666 if you use the Greek spelling of the name, as was done in the eastern part of the empire where John the author of Revelation was writing. If, however, one uses the Latin spelling of Caesar Nero, as was used in the western part of the empire, his name adds up to 616. Significantly, in copies of the book of Revelation that were circulated in the western part of the empire, the number at the end of chapter 13 was changed—to 616.

To early Christians, the meaning of this symbolic number was as plain as a political cartoon would be to people today. Nero, who glorified himself while destroying others, was seen at the time as the personification of the evil of the empire; for it was Nero who had actually started the Roman persecution of the Christians.

The whole empire now—the beast—was embodying the evil of Nero, as it was continuing the persecutions.

The situation in the Roman Empire continues to be depicted in great detail, as chapter 13 describes the actions of the beast. It is said that the beast blasphemes God. The emperors were uttering blasphemy as they claimed divine status. It is said that the beast was making war on the saints. This is exactly what the empire was doing. It is said that the beast would have authority over many peoples and that the inhabitants of the earth would worship it. The inhabitants of the empire were in fact being required to worship the emperor. Then the vision goes on to speak of a second beast that has horns like a lamb—it has the guise of a good religious leader like Christ the lamb—but it speaks like a dragon, speaking words of evil. This second beast would support the worship of the first. Here was a clear reference to the imperial priesthood across the empire that was supporting the whole practice of emperor worship.

What then was the mark of the beast? The word for "mark" is the Greek word *charagma,* which was the word used to designate the picture of the emperor on coins in that day. It is said that the mark of the beast would include his name and his number. Coins did contain the emperor's name along with divine titles attributed to him. The simple message here is that Christians would end up facing economic hardship if they resisted the emperor.

In short, the entire vision of the beasts is not a prediction of future demonic figures about which one can speculate endlessly. The vision is a depiction of the power of evil as it was expressing itself in the Roman Empire. It is precisely at this juncture, however, that the vision can speak to the modern world; because although the vision applied first of all to the first century, it also has had a way of repeating itself in every age. The beast—the power of evil in opposition to God, the "spirit of antichrist"—emerges continually in new forms. As the tenth-century monk Adso put it, "Even now in our own time, we know there are many antichrists."[xi]

The "beast" is in no way a supernatural figure. It has "a human number" (Revelation 13:18). It is human evil and cruelty going against God. This, however, does not make it any less frightening. One has only to look at terrorist attacks today to see that the beast is very much present in our world and that the evil of people who oppose the Spirit of God can be truly horrible.

What can the faithful do in the face of such beastly evil? The message of these chapters about the beasts is finally encapsulated in a single verse which says, "This is a call for the endurance and faith of the saints." (Revelation 13:10) In the face of the beast, Revelation says: keep trusting in God, and join with the Spirit of God in diligently resisting evil; for though the beasts may rage, and though evil may seem at times unstoppable, it is the Lord who rules. Martin Luther summed up this confidence of faith in his classic hymn, "A Mighty Fortress Is Our God" —

"And though this world with devils filled should threaten to undo us,

We will not fear, for God hath willed, his truth to triumph through us."[xii]

THE VERDICT THAT MATTERS
REVELATION CHAPTERS 14 AND 15

Then I looked, and there was the Lamb, standing on Mount Zion! And with him were one hundred forty-four thousand who had his name and his Father's name written on their foreheads. And I heard a voice from heaven like the sound of many waters and like the sound of loud thunder; the voice I heard was like the sound of harpists playing on their harps, and they sing a new song before the throne and before the four living creatures and before the elders. No one could learn that song except the one hundred forty-four thousand who have been redeemed from the earth. It is these who have not defiled themselves with women, for they are virgins; these follow the Lamb wherever he goes. They have been redeemed from humankind as first fruits for God and the Lamb, and in their mouth no lie was found; they are blameless.

Then I saw another angel flying in midheaven, with an eternal gospel to proclaim to those who live on the earth—to every nation and tribe and language and people. He said in a loud voice, "Fear God and give him glory, for the hour of his judgment has come; and worship him who made heaven and earth, the sea and the springs of water." Then another angel, a second, followed, saying, "Fallen, fallen is Babylon the great! She has made all nations drink of the wine of the wrath of her fornication." Then another angel, a third, followed them, crying with a loud voice, "Those who worship the beast and its image, and receive a mark on their foreheads or on their hands, they will also drink the wine of God's wrath, poured unmixed into the cup of his anger, and they will be tormented with fire and sulfur in the presence of the holy angels and in the presence of the Lamb. And the smoke of their torment goes up forever and ever. There is no rest day or night for those who worship the beast and its image and for anyone who receives the mark of its name." Here is a call for the endurance of the saints, those who keep the commandments of God and hold fast to the faith of Jesus.

(cont.)

And I heard a voice from heaven saying, "Write this: Blessed are the dead who from now on die in the Lord." "Yes," says the Spirit, "they will rest from their labors, for their deeds follow them." Then I looked, and there was a white cloud, and seated on the cloud was one like the Son of Man, with a golden crown on his head, and a sharp sickle in his hand! Another angel came out of the temple, calling with a loud voice to the one who sat on the cloud, "Use your sickle and reap, for the hour to reap has come, because the harvest of the earth is fully ripe." So the one who sat on the cloud swung his sickle over the earth, and the earth was reaped. Then another angel came out of the temple in heaven, and he too had a sharp sickle. Then another angel came out from the altar, the angel who has authority over fire, and he called with a loud voice to him who had the sharp sickle, "Use your sharp sickle and gather the clusters of the vine of the earth, for its grapes are ripe." So the angel swung his sickle over the earth and gathered the vintage of the earth, and he threw it into the great wine press of the wrath of God. And the wine press was trodden outside the city, and blood flowed from the wine press, as high as a horse's bridle, for a distance of about two hundred miles.

Then I saw another portent in heaven, great and amazing: seven angels with seven plagues, which are the last, for with them the wrath of God is ended. And I saw what appeared to be a sea of glass mixed with fire, and those who had conquered the beast and its image and the number of its name, standing beside the sea of glass with harps of God in their hands. And they sing the song of Moses, the servant of God, and the song of the Lamb: "Great and amazing are your deeds, Lord God the Almighty! Just and true are your ways, King of the nations!

Revelation 14:1–15:3

In the year 165 AD, a leading Christian by the name of Justin, together with several Christian companions, was brought before the Roman prefect, Rusticus. The brief trial that ensued was recorded in ancient documents. Rusticus inquired first as to whether Justin and his companions were Christians, and when they responded that they were, Rusticus proceeded with a series of threats, designed to move them to renounce their faith and give worship to the Roman gods. They refused. Incredulous, Rusticus made clear that if they did not burn the incense of Roman worship, they would be flogged and beheaded. Still, Justin and his friends remained steadfast. They were executed that day. Justin has henceforth been known as Justin Martyr — one of many early Christians who refused to give up their faith, even under the penalty of death.[xiii]

The trial of Justin Martyr, while it was several decades after the writing of the book of Revelation, was precisely the kind of situation that was being addressed by the book, as the persecutions of Christians by the Roman Empire had started in the late first century.

In such cases, it would have been simple for a person to avoid punishment. The accused could be acquitted by declaring a curse upon Christ and offering a Roman sacrifice, which consisted merely of a pinch of incense placed in a fire that was burning to the honor of the Roman gods. That was all that one had to do! How tempting it would have been to just say a few words, put the sacrifice in the fire, and go free.

The pressure was intense. It would take enormous courage and self-sacrifice to stand up publicly for one's faith; while on the other hand it was very easy, and perhaps would have appeared prudent, to go ahead and deny Christ in order to save one's skin.

This was the circumstance of the Christians to whom the book of Revelation was addressed; and it is this context that the words of chapter 14 resounded with a clear and bold message. An angel is shown flying with an eternal gospel to proclaim, and the angel shouts with a loud voice, saying: "Fear God, and give *God* glory, for the hour of *His* judgment has come, and worship Him who made heaven and earth." (Revelation 14:7) Here was a clarion call to fear and honor and worship God alone, and to be concerned about *God's judgment.* This was followed shortly in the vision by another angel who proclaimed in a loud voice: "If anyone worships the beast"—the beast symbolizing the Roman Empire—"that person shall drink the wine of God's wrath, poured unmixed into the cup of God's anger, and shall be tormented with fire and sulfur." (Revelation 14:9–10) Here was blunt encouragement not to worship the gods of the empire! One should be concerned above all about God's judgment. The section concludes: "This is a call for the endurance of the saints." (Revelation 14:12)

The book of Revelation thus brought a strong admonition to Christians *not to compromise their faith.* At times, the warnings in Revelation may strike the modern reader as severe, yet one must recognize the critical nature of the times. If Christians in those early centuries had buckled *en masse* under the pressure and had denied Christ, the gospel message would have lost its integrity. Who would have followed a religion where everybody bailed out under pressure? On the other hand, the fact that many Christians did not deny Christ but put their lives on the line for their faith spoke powerfully for the truth of the gospel. It was to this faithful endurance that the book of Revelation enjoined its readers.

Times have certainly changed since the days of Justin. Yet in some ways the modern situation is similar to that of Justin, in that Christians today are under pressure to compromise or abandon their faith. In some countries, Christians face extreme social pressures, even to the point of death. In Western society, the pressure is far more subtle, coming from the practices and attitudes of the surrounding society. It is the pressure to abandon moral commitments, become lax in worship, and adopt the materialistic values of the age. No matter what the circumstances, the result of compromise is always negative—a diminishing of faith and an undermining of the church's witness to the world.

While part of chapter fourteen warns against such compromise, other parts offer a more positive remedy to the world's pressures, as believers are encouraged to keep their eye on the goal. This is what moved Justin Martyr and others like him. They kept their eye on the promise of heaven. This promise is depicted in wondrous terms in both chapters fourteen and fifteen in visions of the saints in glory.

Chapter fourteen begins with an image of the 144,000—the people of God in heaven. Chapter fifteen begins with a vision of "those who had conquered the beast ... standing beside the sea of glass with harps in their hands." (Revelation 15:2) Here is one of the most famous visions of heaven—that everyone has a harp! Concerning the 144,000, it is also said that they are those "who have not defiled themselves with women." (Revelation 14:4) Not only does this seem rather sexist, but it appears that there will be quite an unusual and limited group in heaven—144,000 celibate male harpists! Of course, this is one more instance where the imagery in Revelation is meant to be understood symbolically! Along with the symbolic meaning of 144,000—representing the full number of the people of God—the harp in Revelation is a symbol representing beautiful and joyous worship. But what is to be said about the image that these people of God gathered in heavenly worship are those who "have not defiled themselves with women"? In Biblical prophecy, fornication is often an image for *idolatry*—the idea being that people abandon their rightful partner, the Lord, and run after false gods. Thus the image of these people as "undefiled" is a symbolic way of saying that the people in heaven are those who have not defiled themselves with false gods. In short, they have not worshipped the gods of Rome, or the false gods of any age, which was precisely the concern of Revelation 14.[xiv]

The basic situation of early Christians was that they were both literally and figuratively on trial for their faith. The book of Revelation encouraged the faithful to remember *the verdict that matters*. It is God's verdict pronouncing eternal salvation that opens the way into a glorious future. Christians were thus encouraged not to be intimidated by earthly pressures and imperial courts but to hold fast in their faithfulness to God.

The choice between two verdicts receives an additional illustration at the end of chapter 14, in verses 14 to 20, in the vision of the two reapers. One is the grim reaper, who swings a sharp sickle and throws the harvest into the wine press of the wrath of God that sends forth a great flow of blood. The grim reaper is a symbol of the death and destruction coming toward all. But another reaper is also pictured: one like a Son of Man, seated on a white cloud with a golden crown; he brings in God's harvest of life. It is a symbol of the joyous ingathering of all God's people to heaven. As the voice from heaven proclaimed, "Blessed are the dead who die in the Lord." (Revelation 14:13)

Early Christians realized that they stood before something far greater than the verdict of earthly magistrates, who could execute or set free. The verdict that mattered was God's, determining one's everlasting destiny. No matter what the pressures of life, the critical choice—then and now—is to stand firm in faith; for the faithful will join in that joyous song of heaven: "Great and amazing are your deeds, Lord God the Almighty! Just and true are your ways, King of the ages!" (Revelation 15:3)

AN END TO EVIL
REVELATION CHAPTERS 16 AND 17

Then I heard a loud voice from the temple telling the seven angels, "Go and pour out on the earth the seven bowls of the wrath of God." So the first angel went and poured his bowl on the earth, and a foul and painful sore came on those who had the mark of the beast and who worshiped its image. The second angel poured his bowl into the sea, and it became like the blood of a corpse, and every living thing in the sea died. The third angel poured his bowl into the rivers and the springs of water, and they became blood. And I heard the angel of the waters say, "You are just, O Holy One, who are and were, for you have judged these things; because they shed the blood of saints and prophets, you have given them blood to drink. It is what they deserve!" And I heard the altar respond, "Yes, O Lord God, the Almighty, your judgments are true and just!"

The fourth angel poured his bowl on the sun, and it was allowed to scorch them with fire; they were scorched by the fierce heat, but they cursed the name of God, who had authority over these plagues, and they did not repent and give him glory. The fifth angel poured his bowl on the throne of the beast, and its kingdom was plunged into darkness; people gnawed their tongues in agony, and cursed the God of heaven because of their pains and sores, and they did not repent of their deeds.

The sixth angel poured his bowl on the great river Euphrates, and its water was dried up in order to prepare the way for the kings from the east. And I saw three foul spirits like frogs coming from the mouth of the dragon, from the mouth of the beast, and from the mouth of the false prophet. These are demonic spirits, performing signs, who go abroad to the kings of the whole world, to assemble them for battle on the great day of God the Almighty. ("See, I am coming like a thief! Blessed is the one who stays awake and is clothed, not going about naked and exposed to shame.") And they assembled them at the place that in Hebrew is called Harmagedon.The seventh angel poured his bowl into the air, and a loud voice came out of the temple, from the throne, saying, "It is done!" And there came flashes of lightning, rumblings, peals of thunder, and a violent earthquake, such as had not occurred since people were upon the earth, so violent was that earthquake. The great city was split into three parts, and the cities of the nations fell. God remembered great Babylon and gave her the wine-cup of the fury of his wrath. And every island fled away, and no mountains were to be found; and huge hailstones, each weighing about a hundred pounds, dropped from heaven on people, until they cursed God for the plague of the hail, so fearful was that plague.

Revelation 16:1–21

Then one of the seven angels who had the seven bowls came and said to me, "Come, I will show you the judgment of the great whore who is seated on many waters, with whom the kings of the earth have committed fornication, and with the wine of whose fornication the inhabitants of the earth have become drunk." So he carried me away in the spirit into a wilderness, and I saw a woman sitting on a scarlet beast that was full of blasphemous names, and it had seven heads and ten horns. The woman was clothed in purple and scarlet, and adorned with gold and jewels and pearls, holding in her hand a golden cup full of abominations and the impurities of her fornication; and on her forehead was written a name, a mystery: "Babylon the great, mother of whores and of earth's abominations." And I saw that the woman was drunk with the blood of the saints and the blood of the witnesses to Jesus. When I saw her, I was greatly amazed.

But the angel said to me, "Why are you so amazed? I will tell you the mystery of the woman, and of the beast with seven heads and ten horns that carries her. The beast that you saw was, and is not, and is about to ascend from the bottomless pit and go to destruction. And the inhabitants of the earth, whose names have not been written in the book of life from the foundation of the world, will be amazed when they see the beast, because it was and is not and is to come. "This calls for a mind that has wisdom: the seven heads are seven mountains on which the woman is seated; also, they are seven kings, of whom five have fallen, one is living, and the other has not yet come; and when he comes, he must remain only a little while. As for the beast that was and is not, it is an eighth but it belongs to the seven, and it goes to destruction. And the ten horns that you saw are ten kings who have not yet received a kingdom, but they are to receive authority as kings for one hour, together with the beast. These are united in yielding their power and authority to the beast; they will make war on the Lamb, and the Lamb will conquer them, for he is Lord of lords and King of kings, and those with him are called and chosen and faithful." And he said to me, "The waters that you saw, where the whore is seated, are peoples and multitudes and nations and languages. And the ten horns that you saw, they and the beast will hate the whore; they will make her desolate and naked; they will devour her flesh and burn her up with fire. For God has put it into their hearts to carry out his purpose by agreeing to give their kingdom to the beast, until the words of God will be fulfilled. The woman you saw is the great city that rules over the kings of the earth."

Revelation 17:1–18

The story is told of an old man who had worked for years as the custodian of a large building. He was a largely uneducated man, having never completed high school, but he was known for the fact that during his lunch breaks he would often read the Bible. One day as he sat reading a fellow walked by and said, "Hey, what are you reading?" The janitor replied, "I'm reading the book of Revelation." "The book of Revelation!" the other fellow said. "That's a difficult book. Do you understand it?" "Sure," said the custodian, "I understand it." "Well," said the other fellow, "what does it mean?" The custodian replied, "It means, Jesus is gonna win."

That custodian got it right, because if the message of the book of Revelation were to be summed up in one short sentence, the words, "Jesus is gonna win," would pretty well do it. What the book of Revelation declares through all its manifold images is that against the frightening evils of the world, Jesus will ultimately triumph and will bring his people to victory.

The message that first-century Christians heard from the book of Revelation was exactly this message that the old custodian gleaned: Jesus will win! Although the empire in its evil and its power appeared to be invincible, it was Christ who would finally triumph. The message is summed up in chapter 17, verse 14: "They [the forces of evil] will make war on the Lamb, and the Lamb will conquer them, for he is Lord of lords and King of kings."

It must be noted that this was not an easy message to believe during the late first century, when the pagan leadership of Rome was all-powerful and the persecutions could be fierce. It is often not easy to believe that good will really triumph over evil. Yet, the message to the early church came to pass. The persecutions ended; and, in the early fourth century, the emperor, Constantine, became a Christian. Subsequently, Christianity became the dominant religion in the territory of the Roman Empire. In short, Jesus won.

It is striking to note, however, that Jesus won over the evil of Rome in a fashion that many people did not expect. Many early Christians expected that God would finally end the evil of Rome by bringing an overwhelming, supernatural destruction upon the Empire. Instead, in the years following the first century, God *converted* the empire—a very different kind of move! God finally eliminated the persecution and evil of pagan Rome not through destruction, but by overcoming it with good, transforming the empire according to Christian faith.

This says something extremely important about how the Lord might deal with evil today. In recent decades, numerous end-times predictors have claimed that God is about to end the evil of the world by raining supernatural destruction on evildoers and bringing this age to a close. There have been people through centuries past who have sounded this same doomsday trumpet. The imagery in the book of Revelation is often used to try to support these arguments that a violent end of the world is at hand. Yet the fact that these end-times predictors have always proved wrong should lead one to wonder whether there is something amiss with the whole line of interpretation. Moreover, there appears to be a fundamental contradiction between this expectation that God is about to blast an evil world with violence and the ideas of the rest of the New Testament. When Jesus came, many people had expected a warlike Messiah—someone who would smash the evil of the world with violence—but Jesus came as the prince of peace; and if there is anything that Jesus demonstrated on the cross, it is that *the Lord meets and defeats evil through self-giving love.*

It is true that parts of the book of Revelation, such as the bowls of wrath sequence in Revelation 16, portray images of violence. The bowls of wrath images, which reflect the plagues of Egypt, certainly indicate that God is angered at sin, and that God in judgment will allow violence to fall back upon evildoers. One can see this happening throughout history. The bombs that rained on Hitler's Berlin were reminiscent of the hundred-pound hailstones raining on the wicked (Revelation 16:21), and the physical and political destruction of Rome in the fifth century by the barbarians, due to Rome's corruption at the time, was reminiscent of the destruction of "Babylon" that will be described in Revelation chapter 18. One need not suppose that God deals gently with evil; evildoers have repeatedly ended up with bowls of disaster poured upon them.

Evil often sows violence, and in the judgment of God may finally reap violence and disaster upon itself. Yet it is significant that in the visions in Revelation, the real victory over evil does not happen in chapter 16—the violent bowls of wrath chapter—which concludes with people still cursing God. The victory happens in chapter 17, where it is said that the wicked of the world are conquered *by the Lamb*. The image of Christ as conquering Lamb is one of the central and most significant images in the book of Revelation. The lamb recalls the sacrificial Passover Lamb and the way in which Christ gave of himself on the cross to win the victory over sin. The image of conquering Lamb declares that Christ will conquer evil in the way that he conquered it on the cross—defeating evil through self-giving, redemptive love and the proclamation of his truth and peace. Christ will conquer evil by changing people and bringing sinners into the kingdom. That in fact is how Christ defeated the evil of ancient Rome. That also is how Christ has overcome evils across twenty centuries, and it is what Christ is doing today.

The power of evil is often intimidating. In Revelation, this is depicted not only in "the beast" but in the picture of the woman riding the beast who is identified as "Babylon the great—mother of whores and of earth's abominations." (Revelation 17:5) She is also identified as "the great city that rules over the kings of the earth." (Revelation 17:18) In Old Testament times, Babylon was the massive, intimidating capital city of the oppressive Babylonian Empire, which was full of sinfulness, and which conquered Jerusalem, razed the temple, and carried the people into exile.

First-century Jews and Christians readily identified Rome as the *new Babylon*—the all-powerful city at the heart of an oppressive empire, unmindful of God, filled with vices, crushing the downtrodden, and drunk with wealth and power. There are Babylons in today's world as well—wherever sinfulness and power coalesce to oppress the righteous and perpetrate evil. How are Christians to live in the face of such evil, and what will God finally do about Babylon?

End-times predictors say that Christ is going to deal with this Babylon world by coming soon with vengeance to obliterate it all. There is little for the faithful to do now except wait for the bowls of wrath to pour out on all the sinners. But Revelation's image of Christ as conquering Lamb says that Christ is dealing with the Babylon world of today in the same way that Christ dealt with the Babylon of ancient Rome. Christ is seeking to *transform* a wayward world through the forgiveness of the cross. Christ is seeking the renewal of lost people and their inclusion into the kingdom of God. This means that Christ's followers have a calling—not to wait for the doom of the wicked, but to share with Christ in the work of transforming the world, so that the evils of today can be swept aside as surely as the evils of ancient Rome.

"Jesus is gonna win." That promise is sure; and the truly good news is that this victory will come not through destruction but through the redeeming love and transformative power of Jesus Christ.

THE BATTLE OF ARMAGEDDON

REVELATION CHAPTERS 18 AND 19

Then I heard what seemed to be the voice of a great multitude, like the sound of many waters and like the sound of mighty thunderpeals, crying out, "Hallelujah! For the Lord our God the Almighty reigns. Let us rejoice and exult and give him the glory, for the marriage of the Lamb has come, and his bride has made herself ready; to her it has been granted to be clothed with fine linen, bright and pure" — for the fine linen is the righteous deeds of the saints. And the angel said to me, "Write this: Blessed are those who are invited to the marriage supper of the Lamb." And he said to me, "These are true words of God." Then I fell down at his feet to worship him, but he said to me, "You must not do that! I am a fellow servant with you and your comrades who hold the testimony of Jesus. Worship God! For the testimony of Jesus is the spirit of prophecy."

Then I saw heaven opened, and there was a white horse! Its rider is called Faithful and True, and in righteousness he judges and makes war. His eyes are like a flame of fire, and on his head are many diadems; and he has a name inscribed that no one knows but himself. He is clothed in a robe dipped in blood, and his name is called The Word of God. And the armies of heaven, wearing fine linen, white and pure, were following him on white horses. From his mouth comes a sharp sword with which to strike down the nations, and he will rule them with a rod of iron; he will tread the wine press of the fury of the wrath of God the Almighty. On his robe and on his thigh he has a name inscribed, "King of kings and Lord of lords." Then I saw an angel standing in the sun, and with a loud voice he called to all the birds that fly in midheaven, "Come, gather for the great supper of God, to eat the flesh of kings, the flesh of captains, the flesh of the mighty, the flesh of horses and their riders — flesh of all, both free and slave, both small and great." Then I saw the beast and the kings of the earth with their armies gathered to make war against the rider on the horse and against his army. And the beast was captured, and with it the false prophet who had performed in its presence the signs by which he deceived those who had received the mark of the beast and those who worshiped its image. These two were thrown alive into the lake of fire that burns with sulfur. And the rest were killed by the sword of the rider on the horse, the sword that came from his mouth; and all the birds were gorged with their flesh.

Revelation 19:6–21

The Battle of Armageddon is one of the most oft-cited images in the book of Revelation. Armageddon connotes a massive, devastating conflict which lays waste to the earth. Political commentators often use "Armageddon" to denote a military holocaust such as a nuclear war, and the name was even appropriated by a 1998 movie about an asteroid hurtling toward the earth!

The name "Armageddon" appears only once in the Bible and only once in the book of Revelation—in chapter 16, verse 16, which describes the forces of evil assembling for battle "at a place that in Hebrew is called Armageddon." Not much is said of this battle in the subsequent verses. The focus is on the judgment that is coming upon evil. The proclamations of judgment culminate in chapter 18, which is a dirge over Babylon that begins "Fallen, fallen is Babylon the great!" (Revelation 18:2) The first readers of the book of Revelation would have quickly identified "Babylon" as Rome, and would have understood this chapter to be an astonishing declaration that although the persecuting power of Rome seemed invincible, it would be undone by the power of God. Later Christians, experiencing "Babylon" in new forms, have likewise found hope in the declaration that no matter how overwhelming evil may appear, the victory will belong to God.

It is in the latter half of chapter 19 that there is finally a description of a great battle against evil. The forces of God are led by a rider on a white horse, who is obviously Christ. Together with his followers, he battles against the forces of evil and soundly defeats them. Although this battle is not named in chapter 19, it is now generally called the Battle of Armageddon, based on Revelation 16:16.

End-times predictors have typically imagined this to be a literal battle—that there will actually be a final great world battle between the forces of good and the forces of evil at a place in Israel called Armageddon, a battle which will bring this age of human history to a close, and which will conclude with the victorious advent of Christ. It is even sometimes suggested that this will be a nuclear war, which will destroy the earth, after which God will create and new and perfect world.

This whole idea of a literal Battle of Armageddon has been advanced with such fervor in recent years that many people assume it is the only possible interpretation of this passage, and the idea has some significant consequences. The popular view expects the modern state of Israel to be on the good side of the conflict, which is why many churches that hold this understanding are unqualified supporters of Israel. The idea has further consequences when it comes to the issue of working for peace in the Middle East. If a cataclysmic war is inevitable, even God-ordained, it would appear pointless and even against God's plan to be trying to work for peace. The only course would seem to be a resignation to the coming holocaust. One writer, John Wesley White, in a book entitled, *World War III—Signs of the Impending Battle of Armageddon*, put it this way: "The Scriptures teach that the Middle East conflict cannot be settled, and will not be settled, until Jesus Christ comes again."[xv]

The belief in a literal, God-ordained Battle of Armageddon might even make cataclysmic war more likely. During the 1980's, there was concern when President Reagan voiced his belief that there would be a literal, prophesied Battle of Armageddon, perhaps in the near future. Might such a president be more inclined to press the nuclear button, in the belief that he was acting in concert with God? Might such a president be at least disinclined to work for disarmament, in the belief that a nuclear arsenal is a part of God's plan?[xvi] Jerry Falwell encapsulated the view of many prognosticators at the time when he declared that according to his understanding of the Scriptures, Russia was going to attack

Israel in the near future, and the result would be world nuclear war.[xvii]

Robert Jewett, New Testament professor at Garrett–Evangelical Seminary (a United Methodist seminary associated with Northwestern University), responded to such thinking by raising great concern about the implications of what he called the "doom boom"—the popularity of end-of-the-world expectations. He wrote: "My conviction is that the theology of the doom boom is making a decisive contribution to the drift toward a self-imposed Armageddon. When a people become convinced that a holocaust is inevitable and even in the long run desirable because of the new heaven and new earth which will be brought in its stead, the will to resist destruction is eliminated."[xviii] The understanding that one has of the book of Revelation can have real consequences.

Belief in a literal battle of Armageddon, perhaps coming soon, continues to be strong in many churches. But is the imagery of a battle in Revelation 19 intended to be understood literally? The whole chapter in fact is filled with symbolism. Christ leads the battle on a horse—a bit anachronistic for a battle at the present time—and he fights with a sword that comes out of his mouth, which is an image rather difficult to take literally! Moreover, the battle takes place, based on the reference in 16:16, at a place called *Armageddon.*

The name, Armageddon, is a transliteration of the Hebrew phrase, *"Har Megiddo"* (הר מגידו) which means "mountain of Megiddo." There is an ancient town in northern Israel called Megiddo, which was located at a key spot on an ancient trade route and which consequently was the site of some significant historical battles. "Megiddo" thus called to mind for the ancient reader a place of conflict. Megiddo is located, however, on a plain. There are two references in the Old Testament to "the plain of Megiddo." (II Chronicles 35:22; Zechariah 12:11) There is no such place as the mountain of Megiddo. To say that something is going to happen at the mountain of Megiddo is tantamount to saying that something is going to happen on the coast of Nebraska. It is a nonsensical phrase, which is a clue, scholars suggest, that this is not meant to be understood literally! The "mountain of Megiddo" appears rather to be a symbol for a place of fighting and struggle. The Biblical scholar J. W. Bowman put it this way: "As no Mount Megiddo is known to either ancient or modern geographers, it appears the more likely that in a book abounding in symbolical language this term also should be meant to carry a symbolical meaning."[xix]

It is notable that throughout the New Testament, there is re-peated use of the image of warfare to represent spiritual conflict and struggle. In Paul's letters, for example, he speaks of "putting on the armor of God" (Ephesians 6), "fighting the good fight of faith" (I Timothy 6), and suffering hardship "as a good soldier of Christ" (II Timothy 2); and in II Corinthians he says, "We are not carrying on a worldly war, for the weapons of our warfare are not worldly but have divine power to destroy strongholds." (II Cor. 10:3-4) Paul's warfare language is clearly meant to be understood symbolically, and the same must be said of Revelation 19. When it says that Christ carries on the battle with a sword that issues *from his mouth,* this is obviously not meant literally but is a way of saying that Christ carries the spiritual battle through His Word. As the Yale New Testament scholar Paul Minear ob-served, "The only force utilized by the rider on the white horse is the sword of his mouth."[xx] The battle in Revelation 19 is thus rightly understood not as a literal battle with modern weapons at some particular spot and time. The "Battle of Armageddon" is a picture of the overarching spiritual battle between Christ and the powers of evil.

Understood in this light, the passage carries a powerful and positive message for life today. Revelation 19 is not a call to pas-sively resign oneself to a coming world-ending war. Quite to the contrary, the passage calls believers to actively align themselves with Christ and to join in that spiritual battle with Christ against the evils of the present time. It is a battle that is to be carried out not with violence but with the word of Christ, which is a word of righteousness, love, and mercy. Here it is significant that chap-ter 19 once again uses the image of Christ as *Victorious Lamb,* declaring plainly that Christ wins the victory through self-giving love and through overcoming strife with peace. All this means that Christians, quite apart from taking a defeatist attitude toward conflict, should be struggling alongside with Christ in order to create a better world. Christians are summoned to the fight... not a worldly battle of hate and violence, but a spiritual battle against hate and violence to create the love and peace of God's kingdom.

Finally, Revelation chapter 19 proclaims that in this spiritual warfare, Christ will ultimately win. The image of the beast being thrown into the lake of fire is a declaration that evil will be destroyed by Christ. Christians can look forward to the ultimate destruction of all evil, but the image also speaks to the fact that Christ is continually triumphing over evil. To first-century Christians, the beast specifically represented the evil of the Roman Empire in its persecution of the faithful. Christ conquered that beast in those early centuries; and so Christians today can expect that Christ will likewise conquer the beasts with which the faithful wrestle in the present age.

The idea of spiritual war presents people ultimately with a choice—as to which side to be on. This choice comes out in a striking set of images in chapter 19, as it depicts two very different feasts. One is the great supper of the birds, where ravenous birds descend upon the wicked and devour their flesh. (Revelation 19:21) It is a graphic symbol of the destruction and death descending upon all who live apart from God. The other feast is the marriage supper of the lamb (Revelation 19:9)—it is an image of joyous fellowship, life, and union in love with Christ. This is the feast to which all are invited!

The book of Revelation is finally a book not of doom but of hope. The book recognizes that human beings are involved in great and sometimes terrifying struggles. But in the midst of the struggle against evil, Revelation urges believers not to take a fatalistic attitude, but rather to put their trust in Christ, and to join with Christ in the great battle for the good aims of God. The book encourages the faithful that even before the battle is won, they can have confidence in the final victory of the Lord, and can join with that heavenly host in singing, "Hallelujah! For the Lord our God the Almighty reigns. Let us rejoice and exult and give him the glory." (Revelation 19:6-7)

THE REIGN OF CHRIST
REVELATION CHAPTER 20

Then I saw an angel coming down from heaven, holding in his hand the key to the bottomless pit and a great chain. He seized the dragon, that ancient serpent, who is the Devil and Satan, and bound him for a thousand years, and threw him into the pit, and locked and sealed it over him, so that he would deceive the nations no more, until the thousand years were ended. After that he must be let out for a little while. Then I saw thrones, and those seated on them were given authority to judge. I also saw the souls of those who had been beheaded for their testimony to Jesus and for the word of God. They had not worshiped the beast or its image and had not received its mark on their foreheads or their hands. They came to life and reigned with Christ a thousand years. (The rest of the dead did not come to life until the thousand years were ended.) This is the first resurrection. Blessed and holy are those who share in the first resurrection. Over these the second death has no power, but they will be priests of God and of Christ, and they will reign with him a thousand years. When the thousand years are ended, Satan will be released from his prison and will come out to deceive the nations at the four corners of the earth, Gog and Magog, in order to gather them for battle; they are as numerous as the sands of the sea. They marched up over the breadth of the earth and surrounded the camp of the saints and the beloved city. And fire came down from heaven and consumed them. And the devil who had deceived them was thrown into the lake of fire and sulfur, where the beast and the false prophet were, and they will be tormented day and night forever and ever.

Then I saw a great white throne and the one who sat on it; the earth and the heaven fled from his presence, and no place was found for them. And I saw the dead, great and small, standing before the throne, and books were opened. Also another book was opened, the book of life. And the dead were judged according to their works, as recorded in the books. And the sea gave up the dead that were in it, Death and Hades gave up the dead that were in them, and all were judged according to what they had done. Then Death and Hades were thrown into the lake of fire. This is the second death, the lake of fire; and anyone whose name was not found written in the book of life was thrown into the lake of fire.

Revelation 20:1–15

C hapter 20 is the most controversial chapter in the book of Revelation, as it has been the subject of widely different schools of interpretation. The controversy has centered on one key idea in the chapter—the idea of the "millennium," the thousand-year period during which Satan is bound and Christ and the saints reign.

The chapter begins with Satan being bound. Satan, the power of evil, is pictured as a dragon who is bound in chains and locked in a bottomless pit, and he remains there a thousand years. This is followed by a picture of Christ and the martyrs living and reigning, again for a thousand years. After the thousand years, Satan is set loose for a time. There is a final battle during which the wicked are destroyed, and the chapter concludes with a description of the last judgment. The central feature of the passage, around which everything revolves, is *the thousand-year reign of Christ.* The thousand-year span is mentioned a total of six times. It should be noted that a "return" of Christ—the Second Coming—is nowhere mentioned in the flow of this chapter. How should all this be interpreted?

One approach is now called *postmillennialism.* The term indicates a belief that Christ will return *after* the thousand-year "reign of Christ." In other words, the Second Coming is identified with the tumult, the final destruction, and Last Judgment at the end of the chapter. A form of this thinking emerged in the early centuries of the church. Some church leaders believed that the thousand years were to be understood as a span that began with the life and resurrection of Christ. When Jesus died on the cross and rose from the dead, Satan was *bound* as described at the beginning of the chapter—the power of evil was defeated through the cross and resurrection. Now Christ reigns with the saints, as depicted in the first part of chapter 20 (verses 4–6). This meant, however, that the clock was ticking. As the year 1000 approached, there was a good bit of consternation that began to spread across Europe. The end of the millennium was approaching, and this seemed to mean that the end of the age, the Second Coming, and the final judgment were at hand. All kinds of end-of-the-world expectations were spinning across Christendom as the calendar turned to the year 1000. Of course, nothing happened.

The historical pattern of end-times calculations is that when one calculation does not work, the next step is to recalculate. Since nothing happened after one thousand literal years, some people began to redefine what exactly the millennium signified. The most significant medieval example of this was Joachim de Fiore, a twelfth-century monk who in recent years was in the American news, when reports circulated that Barack Obama had referred to Gioacchino da Fiore (the Italian form of the name) three times in his campaign speeches. It was a hoax, but Joachim de Fiore has in fact had a major though largely unrecognized influence on American Christianity.

Joachim de Fiore picked up on a basic concept that was embedded in some early thinking about the millennium—that history can be divided into a sequence of ages that are unfolding according to a precise divine plan. The first age was the Old Testament time, the present age is the millennium, and at the end of the millennium will be the Second Coming, ushering in a new age. Joachim de Fiore advanced this scheme in a fashion more explicit and more highly developed than anyone had before. He said that history can be divided into three *tempora* or ages that correspond with the Trinity. The Old Testament time was the age of the Father, the present time is the age of the Son, and the time period to come, representing a transformation of humanity, will be the age of the Holy Spirit. Joachim de Fiore took the symbols of Revelation and sought to interpret them as predictions of the progressive unfolding of this history. Since the thousand-year expectation of his predecessors had expired, he used another image in Revelation to create a revised timeline. In Revelation 11:3, it is said that "the two witnesses will prophecy for one thousand two hundred and sixty days." Verse 2 and some references in the book of Daniel likewise refer to a span of 42 months or three and a half years—1,260 days. Joachim de Fiore took the days as representing years and took the number literally. He thus concluded that the present age will last for 1,260 years from the time of Christ. This age would end about the year 1260 (Joachim died at age 67 in 1202).

The followers of Joachim de Fiore had great expectations for the year 1260, but of course nothing happened then either. Nevertheless, one can always recalculate. The 1,260 year span was re-applied to other schemes. Several prognosticators, such as David Simpson (1808) and Adam Clarke (1825), claimed that the 1,260 years began with the Donation of Pepin in 754–756, which created the Papal States and inaugurated the temporal rule of the Pope. They expected the end of the present age no later than 2016. Everyone missed it!

Postmillennialism took a new course as people abandoned efforts to start the "millennial clock" at some point in the past and began to conclude that the "millennium"—the reign of Christ on earth—was yet to begin; and church leaders began to expect that this could happen through the work of the church! From the seventeenth century onward, church leaders increasingly saw the "kingdom of God" approaching in the gradual improvement of conditions in Europe and America, where Christians were diligently seeking to create a better world. As the gospel spread across the globe, social conditions advanced, and nations became more civilized in their dealings, it seemed that the reign of Christ on earth was gradually arriving. The Kingdom of God was progressively establishing itself in the whole world! This sort of thinking came to its peak in the late nineteenth century. Many Christians expected that goodness and peace would continue to advance until finally, through the devotion of the faithful, Christ's kingdom would genuinely take hold on earth. Many hymns of the period reflected this thought, such as the 1896 hymn which proclaims:

We've a story to tell to the nations, that shall turn their hearts to the right…

For the darkness shall turn to dawning, and the dawning to noonday bright;

And Christ's great kingdom shall come on earth, the kingdom of love and light.[xxi]

It must be noted that the advocates of this theology did not think of themselves as "postmillennialists," did not generally use the term "millennium," and typically envisioned the Kingdom as an indefinite span, not a literal thousand years. What they expected was that the rule of Christ would gradually arrive on earth, ushered in through the dedicated work of the church, and the Second Coming would occur at some distant point after that. The movement was later described as "postmillennial" because it envisioned the Second Coming of Christ as an event *after* the "millennium." Note how this movement had a tremendous optimism about the human prospect. Human beings through faithful effort are bringing about God's Kingdom on earth!

The whole viewpoint came crashing down with World War I. It became painfully evident that humanity is not progressing at all, at least not in moral or spiritual terms. The Christian optimism of the nineteenth century would be replaced in the twentieth century with much more pessimistic views of the human prospect.

This pessimistic view of the world seemed well founded as the twentieth century progressed. Two world wars, the Cold War, Vietnam, terrorism, and rising concern over pollution and then global warming all added to a sense that the world was unraveling. In this context, there was an interesting reemergence of that old fear that something catastrophic would happen at the end of the millennium. As the year 2000 approached, there was an enormous furor over Y2K—the feared collapse of worldwide computer systems as the millennium turned—and this was linked by many end-times preachers to various end-of-the-world predictions. Of course, the actual arrival of the next millennium was just as eventful as it was in the year 1000.

Overall, however, the growing pessimism about the human prospect provided fertile ground for an entirely new understanding of the millennial reign of Christ—an interpretation that is called *premillennialism.* The name refers to the idea that the Second Coming of Christ will take place *before* the "millennium." In the context of Revelation, premillennialism identifies the Second Coming with the arrival of Christ on the white horse in Revelation 19 and a literal "battle of Armageddon," resulting in the binding of Satan. The thousand-year span to follow is envisioned as a literal direct rule of Christ on earth.

The basic view of premillennialism is that the present age is so wretched that it is beyond repair. It is a troubled time that will soon be followed by yet greater trouble. But then Christ will return, Satan will be bound, and a new age will dawn, as Christ reigns for a literal thousand years on earth. Christians need not worry about the great troubles of today's world, for those troubles will soon be supernaturally swept away; and the greater the troubles, the greater the certainty that Christ's millennium is near! Christians can look instead in hope toward that golden millennial age.

Premillennialism began in the nineteenth century and became widespread in the twentieth, but it has historical antecedents, particularly in Joachim de Fiore. Many premillennialists adopted Joachim's ideas that history is to be divided into periods or ages. This concept came to be called *dispensationalism;* the idea is that God has ordained a sequence of "dispensations" or ages, each with a different structure for how human beings are to respond to God, and humanity is now nearing the conclusion of the sequence. All premillennialists also adopted Joachim's basic understanding that the images in Revelation are to be understood as predictions of events that are unfolding through time. Premillennialists generally believe that while a precise date for the Second Coming cannot be fixed, the time is very soon, and the "predictions" of Revelation are rapidly unfolding.

The premillennialist viewpoint is the centerpiece of the Jehovah's Witness and Seventh Day Adventist belief systems, but it has also become broadly adopted in "evangelical" churches across America. There are various forms of premillennialist theory; but the form that is most widely held is *dispensational premillennialism,* which sees human history unfolding in series of divinely ordained ages leading soon to the "millennium." In spite of quibbling over details, virtually all premillennialists understand Revelation 20 as a description of literal events that are about to unfold. Christ will return, Satan will be bound, and Christ will literally reign for a thousand years on earth. At the end of the millennium, there will be a final cataclysm, as Satan is let loose and there is a final great battle between good and evil, and this will conclude with the triumph of Christ, the Last Judgment, and a new heaven and earth.

Yet the attempt to understand Revelation 20 as a chronology of literal events hits some serious logical snags. If Satan were literally locked away in a pit, why would he be let loose again after a thousand years to wreak havoc once more? If Christ were literally reigning on earth for a period of a thousand years, how could it be that at the end of ten centuries of direct rule by Christ, evil would so arise on the earth that all kinds of nations would turn against Christ and would march against him for battle (Revelation 20:8)? Premillennialists generally avoid such questions. There is no explanation for why Satan would be let loose or why Christ would suddenly lose control of his subjects. Moreover, since premillennialists want to understand the "Battle of Armageddon" in chapter 19 as a literal battle in which Christ decisively defeats evil, it is very hard to explain why there needs to be another literal battle of exactly the same sort a thousand years later. Indeed there is disagreement in premillennialist circles as to which battle is to be called the "battle of Armageddon." Then there is the awkward feature in verse four, which says that only those who were beheaded for their faith will rise to life and reign with Christ during the thousand years—a very limited group!

There is, however, one central problem with the premillennialist view. It is the same problem that medieval Christians had when they expected Christ to return around the year 1000. The problem in both systems is that people have ignored the actual meaning of this image for the original audience to which the book was addressed.

As always in the book of Revelation, John was using images well understood by his readers. While many of the images in Revelation are drawn from the Old Testament, the image of a thousand-year span is drawn from John's larger cultural setting. The only Old Testament verse that mentions one thousand years is Psalm 90:4 — "A thousand years in Your sight are like a day" — and this of course has nothing to do with a thousand-year reign. The image of a thousand-year age comes from the wider cultural landscape of the first century, from one of the predominant religions of the ancient near east — Zoroastrianism. Zoroastrianism was the official religion of the Persian Empire that had ruled over the Jewish people for two centuries — from the late sixth to the late fourth centuries BC — and it was still widespread in the East during John's day. (There are about 200,000 Zoroastrians worldwide today.) The Jewish people were very familiar with Zoroastrian ideas. One of the central features of Zoroastrianism was the idea that human history unfolds in thousand-year periods, which are each brought to a close by a salvific figure. Each period involves a basic struggle between good and evil. This was a ready image to picture what John was talking about in Revelation, as the whole book deals with the struggle of the faithful against evil and the promise of a Savior who would bring victory over evil and a bright future.

Does this mean that John was adopting and promoting Zoroastrian beliefs? By no means! For centuries, Christians in the West have used images drawn out of Greco–Roman mythology, such as Cupid, Damocles' sword, or the Sirens' call. These images have broadly understood meanings, and writers and artists can use them without subscribing to Greco–Roman religion! In the same way, John in Revelation used a classic, broadly understood image drawn out of Zoroastrianism in order to illustrate the message of his book. The picture of the 1,000-year age in chapter 20 led John's readers to think of *a long period of struggle between good and evil which would ultimately be resolved by God's Savior* — a perfect image for the message of Revelation!

John's readers knew the Zoroastrian roots of this imagery and understood that they were not being called upon to adopt a Zoroastrian belief system involving a progression of ages and literal thousand-year spans. Oddly, today's premillennialists move much closer to Zoroastrianism in their scheme. It is worth noting that the term "millennium" never appears in the Bible, and the thousand-year span appears only in Revelation chapter 20. The Biblical Word quite clearly is not calling upon Christians to build an entire belief system around the "millennium," and there is no reason to take the thousand years literally.

Throughout the book of Revelation, numbers are never used literally but have clearly established symbolic meanings. The number 1,000 appears earlier in the "144,000," a number which represents 12 (the number of the tribes of Israel) times 12 (the number of disciples) times 1,000 (the whole number of something)—an image for the whole number of the people of God. Now in chapter 20, the number 1,000 again represents *the whole or the complete number of something*. To speak of a thousand-year reign of Christ is to speak simply of the full or complete reign of Christ. The book of Revelation establishes in its early chapters that Christ reigns right now in heaven! Thus the "thousand-year reign" is a picture of this present spiritual reign of Christ. The passage talks further about Christ reigning with the saints who have been raised from the dead, which is precisely what Christ is doing right now in heaven. The image of the beheaded martyrs is a symbol for all those who have been faithful to Christ. The passage thus speaks a strong word of encouragement to all who have faith, declaring that when the faithful die, they will rise to life and share with Christ in the glory of His rule.

The Zoroastrian backdrop of the thousand-year image adds the sense that during this age there will be an extended struggle between good and evil, but it will all culminate with the final victory of God's righteousness. These themes of the struggle against evil and the assurance of God's victory come forth specifically in chapter 20 in the imagery of Satan loosed and a great battle. First-century Christians would have seen their current situation reflected precisely in this symbolism. They felt that evil had been let loose, and they were in a great spiritual battle; but Revelation 20 gave them the assurance that Christ is on the throne, and His victory is sure!

It is in this context that the pictures of Satan being bound or loosed become fully understandable. Within the present reign of Christ, there is, on the one hand, a sense in which Satan is bound. The idea of the "binding of Satan" is rooted in the gospels. In Matthew chapter 12, there is an account of a confrontation between Jesus and the Pharisees during which the Pharisees accuse Jesus of being able to cast out demons because he is in league with Satan. Jesus answers that his ability to heal demonstrates the opposite—that he has *bound* Satan. He says, "How can one plunder a strong man's house unless one first binds up the strong man?" (Matthew 12:29) The Greek word translated "bind" in Matthew 12:29 is exactly the same word that appears in Revelation 20:2—"He seized the dragon... or Satan, and bound him for a thousand years." The clear message is that Christ binds the power of evil; and indeed many of the early theologians of the church emphasized this point that Christ has defeated the devil. This does not mean that evil is eliminated or destroyed, but that its power is restrained by Christ—appropriately symbolized in Revelation's image of Satan chained.

At the same time, however, there are times when Satan "gets loose"—when evil breaks out in a way that wreaks havoc on the earth. The Second World War was certainly such as time, and the current rampages of terrorism are another case of "Satan unbound." Significantly, in verses seven and eight, which picture Satan getting out of prison and deceiving nations across the earth, those nations are referred to as "Gog and Magog." The names Gog and Magog come from the book of Ezekiel, where they symbolically represent a nation or people that acts against God.

The vision is thus a perfect representation of the human condition. There are times when by the power of Christ evil is restrained, and there are times when evil runs amok. Yet over it all, Christ reigns, and it is clear that Christ is finally triumphant.

Believers are thus encouraged to have confidence in Christ; and believers are drawn to serve Christ in faith, for it is through the power of Christ that evil can be bound and chained in the present time. The Duke University New Testament professor James Efird put it this way: "When the servants of Christ are dedicated and devoted entirely to Christ and to God's Kingdom, Satan is bound.... The binding of Satan is something that can happen anytime or anywhere a person makes a total commitment to God and His purposes."xxii

Here it is apparent that one's view of Revelation has significant implications for life in the present day. The premillennialist view basically holds that the present world is irreparable, that things can only get worse, and that the world will only get better when Christ comes and establishes his thousand-year golden age. Since the millennial age is expected to arrive soon, it makes sense to devote one's efforts not toward fixing up the present mess but toward preparing for the age to come.

A Jehovah's Witness, who was going door to door, was once asked what Jehovah's Witnesses felt about trying to improve conditions in the world. What did they think about efforts to eliminate poverty, or to improve agriculture in developing countries, or to advance education, or to create peace among warring factions across the globe? He replied, "If you were in a house that was on fire, would you stay inside to try to fix the dilapidated staircase, or would you get out of the house?" The obvious answer is to get out of the house! He continued, "That is our view of the world. It is a house on fire, ready to collapse, and we are trying to get people out."xxiii

This is the implication of any view of "the millennium" which holds that nothing will truly improve until Christ returns. It leads to escapism. There are a number of believers today, and not just Jehovah's Witnesses, who have been profoundly influenced by premillennialist ideas and who, as a consequence, are ready to give up on the world. They may even find a certain satisfaction in all the traumas on earth, for the chaotic trouble in the world seems to confirm that the end is near. Christians, they think, should spurn efforts for world peace and social betterment and look instead for the millennial age to come. Yet it is with such ideas that the devil is truly set loose! If Christians pull back from today's needs, the world goes further to ruin.

Fortunately, most Christians over the centuries have gotten a very different message from Revelation. They have understood the images of Revelation 20 as symbols of the ongoing reign of Christ—a reign which is in heaven, but a reign which also takes hold on this earth as the faithful respond in devotion to Christ. This is the meaning of the phrase in the Lord's Prayer where Jesus teaches his followers to pray, "Thy kingdom come, thy will be done, on earth as it is in heaven." The Kingdom is not a purely future realm; it is the rule of Christ that can take hold right now in believers and in the world at large.

This general viewpoint is sometimes called *amillennialism,* as it does not think in terms of any sort of literal millennium, whether in the future or the past. The terms *premillennialism, postmillennialism,* and *amillennialism* are actually used primarily by premillennialists, as a way of distinguishing their viewpoint from other historical perspectives. There are few Christians who actively describe themselves as "amillennialists," because they are not thinking in terms of a "millennium" at all—a term which itself is not even Biblical. But this viewpoint—that the reign of Christ is a present spiritual reality—has been the overarching perspective of Christians throughout the history of the church. In the early centuries of the church, this understanding of Revelation was put forth most systematically by St. Augustine, and it continues to be the perspective of Catholic, Orthodox, and most Protestant Christians today, as well as the perspective found in religion department faculty in major universities everywhere.

It is finally a matter of reading Revelation in the way that John and his original audience read it. It would have brought little encouragement to first-century Christians to think that the binding of Satan and the reign of Christ would be something that might happen more than two millennia later. When they read Revelation 20, they saw the message that Christ reigns now and the power of evil can be chained now. There may be times when evil gets loose, as during the Domitian persecution, but Christians could have confidence in the ultimate defeat of evil and the victory of Christ. The call of Revelation is thus not to give up on human history but to place oneself firmly under the reign of Christ, with the assurance that God's goodness and justice will finally prevail.

PEARLY GATES
REVELATION CHAPTER 21 AND 22

Then I saw a new heaven and a new earth; for the first heaven and the first earth had passed away, and the sea was no more. And I saw the holy city, the new Jerusalem, coming down out of heaven from God, prepared as a bride adorned for her husband. And I heard a loud voice from the throne saying, "See, the home of God is among mortals. He will dwell with them as their God; they will be his peoples, and God himself will be with them; he will wipe every tear from their eyes. Death will be no more; mourning and crying and pain will be no more, for the first things have passed away." And the one who was seated on the throne said, "See, I am making all things new." Also he said, "Write this, for these words are trustworthy and true." Then he said to me, "It is done! I am the Alpha and the Omega, the beginning and the end. To the thirsty I will give water as a gift from the spring of the water of life. Those who conquer will inherit these things, and I will be their God and they will be my children. But as for the cowardly, the faithless, the polluted, the murderers, the fornicators, the sorcerers, the idolaters, and all liars, their place will be in the lake that burns with fire and sulfur, which is the second death."

Then one of the seven angels who had the seven bowls full of the seven last plagues came and said to me, "Come, I will show you the bride, the wife of the Lamb." And in the spirit he carried me away to a great, high mountain and showed me the holy city Jerusalem coming down out of heaven from God. It has the glory of God and a radiance like a very rare jewel, like jasper, clear as crystal. It has a great, high wall with twelve gates, and at the gates twelve angels, and on the gates are inscribed the names of the twelve tribes of the Israelites; on the east three gates, on the north three gates, on the south three gates, and on the west three gates. And the wall of the city has twelve foundations, and on them are the twelve names of the twelve apostles of the Lamb. The angel who talked to me had a measuring rod of gold to measure the city and its gates and walls. The city lies foursquare, its length the same as its width; and he measured the city with his rod, fifteen hundred miles; its length and width and height are equal. He also measured its wall, one hundred forty-four cubits by human measurement, which the angel was using.

(cont.)

The wall is built of jasper, while the city is pure gold, clear as glass. The foundations of the wall of the city are adorned with every jewel; the first was jasper, the second sapphire, the third agate, the fourth emerald, the fifth onyx, the sixth carnelian, the seventh chrysolite, the eighth beryl, the ninth topaz, the tenth chrysoprase, the eleventh jacinth, the twelfth amethyst. And the twelve gates are twelve pearls, each of the gates is a single pearl, and the street of the city is pure gold, transparent as glass. I saw no temple in the city, for its temple is the Lord God the Almighty and the Lamb. And the city has no need of sun or moon to shine on it, for the glory of God is its light, and its lamp is the Lamb. The nations will walk by its light, and the kings of the earth will bring their glory into it. Its gates will never be shut by day—and there will be no night there. People will bring into it the glory and the honor of the nations. But nothing unclean will enter it, nor anyone who practices abomination or falsehood, but only those who are written in the Lamb's book of life.

Revelation 20:1–15

Then the angel showed me the river of the water of life, bright as crystal, flowing from the throne of God and of the Lamb through the middle of the street of the city. On either side of the river is the tree of life with its twelve kinds of fruit, producing its fruit each month; and the leaves of the tree are for the healing of the nations. Nothing accursed will be found there any more. But the throne of God and of the Lamb will be in it, and his servants will worship him; they will see his face, and his name will be on their foreheads. And there will be no more night; they need no light of lamp or sun, for the Lord God will be their light, and they will reign forever and ever.

Revelation 22:1–5

Chapter 20 of Revelation concludes with the last judgment, providing the prelude to chapter 21, which portrays the most compete and stunning New Testament vision of eternal life. The chapter describes the "New Jerusalem"—a future realm where people of faith are dwelling with God. This has become for Christians the quintessential picture of heaven, containing a number of the classic elements that are now traditionally associated with heaven.

It is said, for example, that the heavenly city will have streets of gold—a very popular image for heaven! It is also said that the entrance gates, of which there are twelve, will each consist of a single huge pearl—hence the pearly gates. The walls will be constructed of jasper—a green translucent quartz—and the foundations of the walls will be adorned with all kinds of jewels.

There are some people who want to take this as a literal description of heaven. Yet surely it would be strange if the Lord Jesus, who spent his earthly ministry teaching that gold and precious jewels are not important, would then construct his people's eternal home in such a fashion that its most outstanding feature is that it is filled with gold and precious jewels! As with the images throughout Revelation, these images are meant to be understood symbolically. They each communicate something about the nature of heaven, and their meaning can be discerned by noting what these symbols meant to the original first-century audience.

Chapter 21 starts out by saying that in the eternal future that awaits the faithful, the sea will be no more—no more ocean. To most Americans today, the ocean is a symbol of rest, relaxation, and fun—vacation! If you were going to design an imaginative brochure for heaven, you would probably put an ocean in it. But for the peoples in the ancient near east, the ocean was a frightening thing, a region of turbulence and chaos. They saw it as a realm filled with dark and terrifying creatures; indeed at several points in the Bible the sea is used as a symbol for chaos and evil. To say that "the sea is no more" is thus to say that the chaos of sin and evil will be removed.

At the same time, the image of water is used in chapter 21 in a very positive way in symbols of rivers and springs. In the dry lands of the ancient near east, one of the most poignant images of refreshment and renewal was the image of a fresh-water spring or stream. A river flowing through otherwise dry ground would bring abundant life. Significantly, the prophet Ezekiel, speaking of the fulfillment of God's promises, had a vision of a great river flowing from the temple through the midst of God's people (Ezekiel 47). When Revelation says that "the river of the water of life, bright as crystal, flows from the throne of God through the middle of the city..." (Revelation 22:1-2), it is a picture of Ezekiel's river and a powerful declaration that *abundant life* awaits the faithful.

The heavenly city itself is described as *the new Jerusalem*. Since Old Testament times, Jerusalem had been regarded as the holy city—the city of God—the place where God especially dwelled. To speak of the New Jerusalem is thus to speak of a realm where God will be fully present with people. Fittingly, the New Jerusalem is described in these terms: "Behold, the dwelling of God is among people. He will dwell with them as their God, and they will be His people. God himself will be with them." (Revelation 21:3) This is the essence of what heaven is—to be is to be in the joyous and loving presence of God.

The symbolism continues in verse seven in the unusual dimensions of the city. It is said that the city is 12,000 stadia—about fifteen hundred miles—in length, width, and height. In other words, it is a giant, perfect cube. It would be extremely awkward to interpret this literally! But the image makes perfect sense symbolically, since in ancient times the cube was considered to be the most perfect of all geometric figures,[xxiv] and thus it serves as an appropriate image for the perfection of heaven. Moreover, in the Old Testament, there is one place where a cube appears—in the Holy of Holies. The Holy of Holies was small, central room in the temple considered to be the dwelling place of God; it was in the shape of a perfect cube. In Biblical days, the Holy of Holies was entered only once each year by the high priest. Now, however, that cube has expanded! It encompasses the entire new Jerusalem, and God's people are in it continually. The symbolism beautifully proclaims that God's presence will encompass all God's people all the time.

Another interesting feature of the heavenly city is that although it has walls—which were a standard feature in all ancient cities—the gates to the city are said to be open continually. In ancient cities, the gates were shut in times of danger and every night as a security measure. But in the New Jerusalem, the gates are constantly open—indicating a lack of danger and an unbroken accessibility to the presence of God.

Still another piece of symbolism suggesting the experience of the presence of God can be found in the statement that "they will see God's face." (Revelation 22:4) In ancient times, to see the face of the king meant not simply that one managed to catch a glimpse of his highness as he went riding by. To "see the face of the king" meant that one had been granted an audience with the king—an opportunity to speak personally face to face. To "see the face of God" means sharing in an intimate personal relationship with God.

At the same time, this does not mean that eternity will consist solely of a one-to-one relationship between the individual and God. The very image of a city suggests a large community of persons. The New Jerusalem is a fellowship of people who are sharing in love with one another as well as with God.

The materials out of which the city is "constructed" are all symbols of the glory and wonder of this fellowship with God. In ancient times, streets were either not paved at all or were paved with stones; in the New Jerusalem they are paved with gold. In ancient cities, the walls were built out of stone and the gates out of wood and iron. In the heavenly city, the walls and gates consist of jewels. All this is a way of saying that to dwell eternally with God is extraordinarily marvelous! It will be far beyond anything experienced on earth.

There is another interesting feature of the jewels. The gems in the foundations are listed quite carefully in Revelation 21:19–20 and may strike the modern reader as strange, but in ancient times all these gems were quite familiar. The twelve gems listed were twelve gems that were associated at the time with the twelve signs of the Zodiac. Each sign of the Zodiac in ancient times had a corresponding gemstone, just as today each month has a corresponding birthstone. Everyone knew these stones, and there was a standard order in which they would typically be listed along with the chronological order of the Zodiac. But the book of Revelation precisely reverses the order from its usual flow. Biblical scholars suggest that this reversal is meant as a repudiation of astrology.[xxv] John is telling us that the future is not determined by the stars; it is determined by the promises and plans of God.

The whole picture of the new Jerusalem is thus a picture of the destiny of the faithful. It is an everlasting, joyous future with God. This promise would have been an enormous encouragement for first-century Christians under persecution, for it declared that no matter what they endured in the present, their future was bright. At the same time, the picture was not simply that the faithful would enjoy heaven while earth continued to go to ruin. Revelation 21 begins with the words "Then I saw a new heaven and a new earth." (Revelation 21:1) The expectation was that God would act to bring renewal to all of creation. This continues a theme that is found in Old Testament prophets who envisioned a day when the whole earth would be infused with the peace and good will of God. As the prophet Isaiah put it, "The wolf shall live with the lamb, the leopard shall lie down with the kid, the calf and the lion and the fatling together, and a little child shall lead them." (Isaiah 11:6) The apostle Paul likewise looked forward to a time when the whole earth would be set free from the taint of human sinfulness, and all things would be in harmony with God. As he said in

Romans 8, "The creation itself will be set free from its bondage to decay and obtain the glorious liberty of the children of God." (Romans 8:21) Believers are thus called not to abandon concern for planet earth in favor of an otherworldly hope, but to share in God's work for the renewal of all things.

The book of Revelation puts forth a holistic vision of God's power to bring new life, and this vision connects with the whole Biblical story. The phrase "new heaven and new earth" is found earlier in the prophet Isaiah, in chapters 65 and 66, where the prophet was speaking of God's renewing power over all things; and the phase hearkens back to the very beginning of the Bible—"In the beginning God created the heavens and the earth." (Genesis 1:1) The vision of Revelation 21–22 is not simply of a "heaven" as a spiritual place where the faithful go when they die. The vision is that all of creation has a glorious destiny—a fulfillment of what God began at the dawn of creation. The vision thus declares that the universe is not simply adrift, but that God is drawing all things toward a marvelous goal.

At this juncture, people have sometimes gotten entangled in debates about what exactly the "new heaven" is and what exactly the "new earth" is and where the "New Jerusalem" fits in to all this. There is always a temptation to become literalistic about the symbols and to speculate about the details of eternity. Jehovah's witnesses, for example, posit a spiritual heaven made of up 144,000 elite believers and an earthly paradise consisting of the rest of Jehovah's Witnesses. Other commentators will point out that in Genesis 1, "heaven" actually means the realm of sun and stars, and thus the "new heaven and new earth" must indicate simply one renewed universe. People have spun out endless scenarios.

Here it must be noted that the phrase "new heaven and new earth" appears only once in chapter 21, verse 1; the clear point is that God will fulfill what God began at the beginning. The major content of what follows is the vision of the New Jerusalem, where the symbolism is such that it is plainly describing something that is beyond our full comprehension. This means that it is pointless to try to pin down the "what" and the "where" of eternal life with

God. It is helpful to remember that Jesus never gave details about heaven but firmly proclaimed the basic promise of everlasting life. Believers are called not to speculate about eternity but to take hold of ultimate vision of Revelation — that God has opened up a bright and glorious future.

The book of Revelation is a most fitting conclusion to the Bible, as it brings the whole message of the Scripture to a coherent and shining conclusion. The Bible begins with the story of human estrangement, as humanity turns from God in sin. Human beings are now in bondage to decay and death, symbolized in the banishment from the Garden of Eden. The tree of life, at the center of the garden, is never to be seen again throughout the Biblical story. But now, in the final chapter of Revelation, the tree of life appears again! (Revelation 22:2) It is a powerful declaration that God through Christ has answered the problem of sin, overcome human estrangement, and restored humanity to the promise of life abundant and everlasting. This is a promise so glorious it can only be expressed in poetic imagery. Thus the Bible concludes with the brilliant imagery of Revelation, inspiring the faithful to look upon life as a journey by God's grace toward that wondrous, eternal city.

The medieval monk Bernard of Cluny expressed exactly this perspective in his classic poem:

> Jerusalem the golden, with milk and honey blest!
> Beneath thy contemplation, sink heart and voice oppressed.
> I know not, O I know not, what joys await us there;
> What radiancy of glory, what bliss beyond compare.
> O sweet and blessed country, the home of God's elect!
> O sweet and blessed country, that eager hearts expect!
> Jesus, in mercy bring us, to that wondrous land of rest:
> You who are with God the Father and Spirit ever blest.[xxvi]

BEYOND DOOMSDAY

Today in America there is a line of thinking about the "end times" that is so widespread and so oft-repeated that many people assume it must be rooted in the book of Revelation. One hears that we are in the "last days" and that events are unfolding that are fulfilling ancient end-times prophecies. Soon an Antichrist will appear, who will pretend to be a force for world harmony but who will take control of the earth and usher in a time of enormous trouble called the Tribulation. Before the onset of the Tribulation, Christians will be whisked out of the earth through the Rapture—a supernatural event in which they are bodily removed from the earth and taken to heaven. Since the Church will thereby be removed from the planet, God's central instrument during the Tribulation will be the nation of Israel, restored to its final purpose as the people of God in these end times. Ultimately, the forces of evil will move against Israel for the Battle of Armageddon; but Christ will return in glory (the Second Coming) to defeat the Antichrist and all the power of evil, ushering in the Millennium, the thousand year reign of Christ on earth. This will be followed by the final "loosing of Satan" and a last battle and then the Last Judgment and new heaven and earth. With slight variations, this is the basic scenario that is promoted broadly in book and movies, by TV evangelists, and many "evangelical" churches.

The Rapture, which is at the front end of this timeline, is expected soon. Several years ago, bumper stickers could often be seen which read, "In case of Rapture, this car will be unmanned." How this was thought to attract people to Christian faith is unclear; but the plain expectation was that the Rapture could occur at any time! The idea that humanity is on the verge of these last days is reiterated constantly by many end-times preachers. The most popular expression of this whole line of thought was the "Left Behind" book series, also made into a movie, which told a story about people who were "left behind" following the Rapture to face the Great Tribulation.

This entire end-times scenario has major implications. It leads to suspicion toward all efforts to work for world harmony, since the Antichrist is expected to come to power precisely by promising to unite the world. It leads to unconditional support for the nation of Israel, since Israel is believed to be God's chosen instrument for the last days. It leads to a lack of interest in long-term projects to improve the world, since this age is expected to come to a ruinous end soon. And it leads to a complete lack of interest in world peace, since the Battle of Armageddon is considered inevitable and approaching fast.

This end-times scenario has been promoted heavily for decades. In the 1970's, it was especially popularized by Hal Lindsay, whose book *The Late, Great Planet Earth* saw events of the day as the beginning of the "last days" timeline. Many of Lindsay's specific ideas proved wrong, but the basic end-times scheme has been promoted in new variations, to such an extent that many people assume it must be Biblical and that this must be the way to understand the book of Revelation. Few people realize that the entire scenario has its origin in the nineteenth century, in an Irishman by the name of John Darby.

John Nelson Darby was a part of a radical church group in the early 1800's which expected the near-term end of the world. He devised a blueprint of the end times by drawing together verses from here and there in the Bible. His basic approach was to disregard the original setting and meaning of those verses and to piece the verses together according to a plan that emerged out of his own thinking and the ideas of other end-times thinkers of his day. Out of it all he created a scenario that had a certain captivating brilliance and intrigue to it, so that it began to gain popularity. Darby's ideas spread in America particularly through a series of conferences called the Niagara Bible Conferences, which were especially exciting because the speakers had a way of proclaiming that Christ might return before the meeting was over. Of course, before long that rhetoric began to wear a little thin, and the conferences ended. But others picked up on Darby's ideas, such as Dwight L. Moody, whose Moody Bible Institute would become a training ground for Darbyism, and, most notably, Cyrus Scofield. Scofield put out a version of the Bible with notes alongside the King James text of the Bible. The notes explained and interpreted the Bible according to the Darbyist scheme. This version was called the Scofield Reference Bible, and it became the standard Bible used for years in many conservative churches. In other words, people began to read their Bible through the lens of John Darby, so that Darby's scheme became adopted on a broad scale. Nowadays, most people who accept the Darbyist scheme do not even know that their ideas have their origin in John Darby. His system has gained a life of its own. The system is now generally called *dispensational premillennialism,* which was briefly described in chapter 12.

Meanwhile, as Darbyist thinking has dominated the airwaves and the titles of popular religious books, Biblical scholars in universities and seminaries all across the globe have been saying something quite different. It is this scholarship that has been reflected in the pages of this book.

One of the most important principles of Bible study is to read the Bible on its own terms, so that each Biblical passage speaks the message it was intended to say. In Biblical studies, this is called *exegesis*—which means to "read out" the message of each passage. The opposite, false approach is called *eisegesis,* which means to "read in" one's own ideas to shape the Biblical message according to one's own preferences and designs. This is exactly the approach taken by John Darby and his heirs, who thus do what Revelation at the end warns against—adding to or subtracting from the message of the book. (Revelation 22:18–19) The whole approach was rightly described by James Efird as "a matter of playing games with the sacred text."[xxvii]

When the book of Revelation is read on its own terms, the entire Darbyist scheme falls apart. This is particularly clear when considering the popular Darbyist idea of the Rapture. John Darby invented the idea of the "rapture"—as an event separate from the Second Coming when the faithful would be transported out of the world prior to a "tribulation"—around 1827. There is a good reason why the Rapture was never discussed in this volume, except for a passing reference to a Rapture prediction in chapter one. It is because the concept is completely absent from the book of Revelation!

Not only does the book of Revelation never mention any event resembling the Rapture, but the concept itself is completely contradicted by the main idea in the book. John in Revelation never suggests that the faithful will be whisked out of the world before tribulation arrives. To the contrary, he constantly speaks of how the faithful are *in the midst of tribulation*. The answer to that tribulation is not that the faithful will escape it, but that the Lord stands with them in the midst of it, so that they can have confidence in their final deliverance. (For more about the idea of the Rapture, see the appendix below.)

Another major problem with Darbyism is its concept of the role of Israel. In addition to the novel idea of "the rapture," John Darby invented another unique idea in Christian history with his suggestion that the Church and Israel have distinct roles in God's end-times plan. Darby's scheme is that the Church will be removed from the world before the "tribulation," and he argued that God would then work through the Jewish people in "fulfillment" of certain Old Testament prophecies that Darby understood literally and divorced from their actual historical context. Israel would thus be God's prime instrument in the last days. Such thinking is completely absent from the book of Revelation, which speaks of one people of God saved by the Lamb, who are the church—as represented in the seven churches to which Revelation is addressed. This does not mean that God has rejected the Jews—see Paul's letter to the Romans for a discussion of how the Jewish people will yet be included in God's grace—but it precludes any special role for "Israel" in "the last days."

A similar problem appears with the Darbyist concept of the Antichrist—the term never appears in the book of Revelation. Darby wanted to equate the beast in Revelation with an end-times individual (the Antichrist), but in Revelation the beast clearly signifies the empire in John's own day.

Likewise the term "Millennium," the very center of the Darbyist system, never appears in the book of Revelation; and the thousand-year span, mentioned only in one chapter, is not meant to be understood as a literal future reign, but is a clear symbol for the ongoing reign of Christ.

The overarching problem with Darbyism is that it takes symbols that are depictions of the first-century world and wants to make them into literal predictions for today. Additionally, Darbyism mixes and matches symbols from across the Bible, giving them all various literal interpretations, to force a scheme that is utterly foreign to the Biblical message.

A basic problem beneath all this is to be found in the understanding of *prophecy*. The book of Revelation describes itself at multiple points as "prophecy." Today people often want to think of prophecy as a prediction of the future, and this is at the heart of the Darbyist world view. But the prophets of the Bible were not fortune tellers. The word "prophet" means "one who announces," and the role of the prophet was to announce God's Word. Sometimes this would include a general reference to what God would do in the future, but for the most part the prophets declared God's Word for their own day. This can be seen throughout the writings of the Old Testament prophets, and the same holds true for Revelation. The book of Revelation makes reference to the future, but the thrust of the book is to declare God's Word for first-century Christians who were under extreme pressure.

Yet just as the Old Testament prophets, while speaking to their own age, brought a message that applies to every age, so the book of Revelation, while it was addressed to first-century churches, brings a message for today. John had said at the outset that the book describes "what is and what is to come." When reading through the book, it is quite apparent that a great many of the images are *both what is and what is to come*—the images portray ongoing spiritual realities.

While Christians in the first century and Christians today live in very different worlds, on a spiritual level those worlds are quite similar. Evil runs rampant and seems at times to be overwhelming, and people of faith are under great pressure. But the visions of Revelation speak a word of great hope to each age. Visions such as the magnificent vision of the Lord on the throne of heaven (early in the book) declare that the Lord holds the real power in the universe, and therefore the faithful can have confidence in spite of the terrors of the day. Visions such as the vision of the defeat of the beast (in the middle of the book) declare that the Lord is with His people and will ultimately break the rampaging evil that devastates the earth. Visions such as the vision of heaven (at the end of the book) remind Christians that even death has been defeated by the victory of Christ, and that those who put their faith in Christ will be brought through every trial into eternal life. The visions of Revelation thus bring to Christians a message of enormous encouragement in the midst of trial. The book says to believers: do not fear that evil is going to get the upper hand; keep on in faith, share with courage in the good work of God, and know that you are a part of the everlasting victory of the Lord.

Thus the book of Revelation speaks to the present age, not because it is a set of predictions, but because it is a book with a timeless message that has spoken powerfully to Christians in every age. When times are difficult, the book of Revelation would move believers to open the eyes of their hearts to a greater reality—to see that the Lord is on the throne of the universe, to see that the Lord is with the faithful, and to see that the Lord is opening up a bright and eternal future. The vision of Revelation is one that will bring believers in every age into a courageous faith and an abiding hope.

CHRIST IS COMING SOON

The one who testifies to these things says, "Surely I am coming soon." Amen. Come, Lord Jesus! The grace of the Lord Jesus be with all the saints. Amen.

Revelation 22:20–21

In the spring of 2011, billboards began springing up across American announcing Judgment Day on May 21, 2011. The billboards were sponsored by Harold Camping's Family Radio Network. Harold Camping, who preached that all churches are apostate and that only his radio network had the truth, proclaimed specifically that the Rapture would occur on May 21, to be followed by five months of tribulation, culminating with the end of the world on October 21, 2011. When nothing happened, he first tried to insist that some "spiritual" event had occurred; but finally, in March 2012, he wrote, "We humbly acknowledge we were wrong about the timing."

Whether Harold Camping will be the last of the end-times date setters remains to be seen. Yet even as most of today's end-times preachers will avoid date setting, they typically proclaim that Christ is returning very soon. Often preachers announce what has become the standard premillennialist timeline—Christ will spiritually return for His Church (the Rapture), there will then be seven years of Tribulation, and then Christ will physically return to establish His thousand-year reign (the Millennium). One is given the impression that God has an end-times clock that is ticking toward an inexorable and very near-term climax.

Such end-times prognosticators like to quote the second-to-last verse in Revelation—"Surely I am coming soon." (Revelation 22:20, also 22:12) They seem to forget that this verse is over two thousand years old!

In view of the enormous gap between "I am coming soon" in 90 AD and the present date, dispensational premillennialists will often draw on John Darby's teaching that the present age of the church is a "great parenthesis" in God's prophetic time clock. In

137

other words, God stopped the end-times clock for the past two thousand years. Darby needed this "parenthesis" idea to make his literalist interpretations work out—one more example of the kinds of games that end-times predictors play. But now, we are told, the clock is ticking again! Premillennialist preachers will often point to the founding of the state of Israel in 1948 as a key event signaling that the last days are upon us. But Jesus warned about anyone who claims to know God's timing. "Of the day or the hour," said Jesus, "no one knows." (Matthew 24:36)

What then is the modern reader to make of a two-thousand-year-old statement that Jesus is coming soon? One solution, perhaps, is to keep in mind the clearest statement in the Bible about God's timing—"A thousand years to the Lord are like a day." (Psalm 90:4) For the God of the universe, "soon" obviously may mean something different than it means to us! Yet if modern readers must expand the word "soon" into infinity, the statement, "Surely I am coming soon," appears finally to be virtually meaningless. This is why many Christians today simply ignore the verse altogether.

The confusion surrounding this verse has to do entirely with the assumptions that contemporary readers are making about the book of Revelation. When people make the book of Revelation into a prediction of events in the end-times, they inevitably see the statement "Surely I am coming soon" as a reference to the Second Coming of Christ at the end of time. Then they must go through all sorts of gyrations to try to get "soon" to correspond with the passage of two millennia. The situation changes entirely when the book of Revelation is understood on its own terms.

The book was a letter addressed to first-century churches, and therefore it must have had a message for that audience—a community of Christians facing severe pressure during the reign of Domitian. Whenever people are in dire straits, the most important message that they can hear is, "Help is coming soon!" This is exactly the message that the original audience would have heard in the closing verses of the book of Revelation. It would have done them no good to think that the Second Coming might occur in two thousand years or more. When they heard "Surely I am coming soon," they understood it to be a promise that God was coming quickly to their aid.

This, in fact, is what happened. All the churches addressed in Revelation continued to thrive; and although persecutions continued off and on over the next two centuries, the church across the empire grew tremendously, until the Roman Emperor became a Christian (Constantine in the early fourth century). Christ was powerfully at work in those early centuries.

The statement "Surely I am coming soon" was never intended to spur Christians to make predictions about the Second Coming. It was intended to encourage Christians to be receptive to the coming of Christ in the here and now. It thus had the same basic message as the many gospel teachings of Jesus about being ready for the Lord to come. In multiple teachings and parables, such as the parable of the ten bridesmaids or the parable of the faithful servant, Jesus encouraged his followers to be watchful and ready at all times for the entrance of the "bridegroom" or the "master." Believers were called not to speculate about the future but to anticipate how Christ would come with saving power in the present day.

Here is the message of these words for Christians today! "Surely I am coming soon" tells Christians that God will never abandon the church. Even in moments of great distress—such as Christians were experiencing in the first century—believers can have the assurance that the Lord will come with saving help. Thus the final prayer in Revelation—"Come, Lord Jesus!" (Revelation 22:20)—is not a petition asking God to please bring down the curtain on world history; it is a prayer in which the faithful ask Christ to come into their lives with redeeming grace and power.

The book of Revelation concludes with the benediction, "The grace of the Lord Jesus be with all the saints." (Revelation 22:21) It is an appropriate conclusion, for this is the thrust of the whole book—that believers (the saints) might live right now in the grace of Jesus Christ.

HOPE IN A TIME OF CHAOS AND EVIL

We long to know what the future holds. Whether it is stock gurus or weather forecasters or pollsters before an election, those who offer to tell us what is coming find a ready audience. Hence the popularity of those who claim to have figured out God's precise plan for our future.

There has been a huge number of books, TV messages, and internet posts that use the book of Revelation as a prediction of future events. This popular material routinely distorts the book of Revelation in two key ways — (1) passages are interpreted literally that are meant to be symbolic (as in the "thousand years" in chapter 20), and (2) passages that are accepted as symbolic are interpreted without reference to their actual intended meaning (as in the "beast"). The result is a fantasy "future" that has little to do with actual message of the book of Revelation.

This whole approach makes the book of Revelation into a book of doom, and prods people into a fatalistic attitude toward world events. The world as we know it will crash into ruin, the doomsday preachers declare, and the end is near! Harrell F. Beck, a renowned Biblical scholar at Boston University, once remarked that in all the doomsday preaching he had ever heard about the end being upon us, there always still seemed to be time to send in a contribution. He said he would sit up and listen when someone announced, "The end is here; you don't even have time to write a check."[xxviii] That never happened.

The "doom boom" has in fact been a financial boom for a number of end-times prognosticators, but the distortion of the book of Revelation has been a burden for Christians as a whole.

A man in Ohio once called a pastor in town, pleading for the pastor to come to the house and speak to his distressed wife.

Upon arrival, the pastor found the living room full of stacks of laundry. The woman was slumped on the couch. She explained to the pastor that she had lost all motivation to do anything. She had been listening to the preachers on television, who were making clear that the world was about to end. Why do the laundry?[xxix]

She had some deeper issues, but the doomsday view of Revelation was not helping. This is true of the world as a whole—the world has serious issues, and the doomsday view of Revelation is not helping! Christians are being drawn into false and counter-productive thinking, which undermines the real work of God's Kingdom.

The actual message of Revelation is a message that is entirely different from what is so often proclaimed by the end-times prognosticators. The book is not a set of predictions but a profound declaration of how God works in the face of evil. The book brings genuine promise, not by forecasting that God will soon put an end to this world, but by showing what God is doing to redeem the world. The book of Revelation, when rightly understood, provides great reason for hope in a time of chaos and evil.

Anyone looking at today's world could easily despair. But the book of Revelation would open our vision to a greater reality. The images in Revelation are powerful precisely because they can draw us to a heightened spiritual awareness of how God is at work above and beyond all things. The symbols in Revelation bring us into profound spiritual insight *when we let the symbols speak on their own terms.* Then we find that Revelation, far from being a foretelling of a frightful future, is a portrayal of how God is at work to deliver us from evil. The rich imagery in this *apocalypse* declares:

- The world may seem out of control, but the Lord is on the throne—God is in charge!
- The world may seem to be filled with trouble, but there is an ultimate Power in the universe, against which no evil can stand!
- The world may seem chaotic, but there is an ultimate Purpose in the universe, drawing us toward an eternal destiny!

- The world may seem governed by evil, but the Redeeming Love of God prevails over all!

Therefore people of faith today can truly have hope.

In the end, the hope of Revelation is not the passive hope of an audience watching a bad play, just waiting for the curtain to fall. It is the active hope of athletes on the field, engaged in a mighty struggle. The opposition is daunting, and the outcome may appear in doubt; but in fact, victory is assured! So the faithful are encouraged to struggle onward, trusting in the One who leads them, confident in the triumph to come. This was the hope of the Christians who first heard the message of Revelation, and who shared vigorously in advancing the gospel in their time; and it can be our hope today. In spite of the chaos and evil of our age, we can join in God's work and move forward with assurance, because our destiny is in the hands of the One who said, "I am the Alpha and the Omega, the beginning and the end. To the thirsty I will give water without price from the fountain of the water of life. Those who conquer will inherit these things—I will be their God and they will be my children." (Revelation 21:6–7)

APPENDIX: THE RAPTURE

The concept of the Rapture—that the faithful will be supernaturally removed from the world before the onset of a great Tribulation—is popular among many Christians, yet it is entirely absent from the book of Revelation. From where does the concept come? Advocates of the Rapture idea draw on two main Bible passages. In the gospel of Matthew, Jesus says, "As the days of Noah were, so will be the coming of the Son of Man. For as in those days before the flood they were eating and drinking, marrying and giving in marriage, until the day Noah entered the ark, and they knew nothing until the flood came and swept them all away, so too will be the coming of the Son of Man. Then two will be in the field; one will be taken and one will be left. Two women will be grinding meal together; one will be taken and one will be left." (Matthew 24:37–41) Although some now want to see this as a picture of "the Rapture," Biblical scholars will note that to read the passage in this way is to read a modern idea back into the Biblical text. The actual words of Jesus simply indicate a picture of a day of judgment when some are saved (as those on the ark) and some are "swept away." The other Biblical passage often quoted by Rapture advocates is in I Thessalonians, where Paul says, "For this we declare to you by the word of the Lord, that we who are alive, who are left until the coming of the Lord, will by no means precede those who have died. For the Lord himself, with a cry of command, with the archangel's call and with the sound of God's trumpet, will descend from heaven, and the dead in Christ will rise first. Then we who are alive, who are left, will be caught up in the clouds together with them to meet the Lord in the air; and so we will be with the Lord forever." (I Thessalonians 4:15–17) The Rapture concept draws directly on the notion in this passage of believers being "caught up in the clouds to meet the Lord in

147

the air." In the Latin Vulgate translation of this passage, the word for "caught up" is the Latin verb, *rapio,* and it is from this term that the word "rapture" derives. Note, however, that this passage does not assert that believers will be whisked mysteriously out of the world before some great end-times tribulation—the modern Rapture concept. It describes the Second Coming of Christ, and it says that believers alive at the time will be lifted into Christ's eternal presence along with those who have died in faith before. It is meant by Paul as an encouragement to the faithful that we will be joined with loved ones who have gone before us in the glory of heaven. As Paul continued, "Therefore encourage one another with these words." (I Thess. 4:18)

Beyond these two short passages, neither of which actually supports the modern idea of the Rapture, the Rapture concept is absent from the rest of Scripture, and it is completely denied in the book of Revelation. For all its popularity, the modern notion of "the rapture" is unbiblical.

This is why the concept of a pre-tribulation rapture is absent from all of Christian history prior to the 1800's. The "rapture" is an invention of John Nelson Darby, popularized greatly through his successors. Major Biblical scholars routinely point out the serious flaws in the whole rapture idea. For an extended scholarly study on the subject, see Robert Jewett, *Jesus Against the Rapture,* Philadephia: The Westminster Press, 1979.

NOTES

CHAPTER 1
[i]   quoted in Kuwait Times, March 8, 2018

CHAPTER 2
[ii]   Pliny, *Letters,* 10.96
[iii]   Pliny, *Letters,* 10.97
[iv]   Elisabeth Schussler Fiorenza, *The Book of Revelation: Justice and Judgment* (Philadelphia: Fortress Press, 1985), p. 187.

CHAPTER 4
[v]   C. B. Caird, *The Revelation of St John the Divine* (San Francisco: Harper & Row, 1966), p. 75.

CHAPTER 5
[vi]   Richard DeHaan, *Warning: The Horsemen Are Coming* (Grand Rapids, Michigan: Radio Bible Class, 1981), p. 7.
[vii]   Joachim de Fiore, "Letter to All the Faithful," trans. by Bernard McGinn, in *Apocalyptic Spirituality* (New York: Paulist Press, 1979), p. 117.
[viii]   John Wesley, *Explanatory Notes on the New Testament,* Vol. II (Grand Rapids, Michigan: Baker Book House, 1981), comment on Rev. 6:8.

CHAPTER 6
[ix]   Tertullian, *Apology,* 40.2.

CHAPTER 7
[x]   James M. Efird, *End-Times* (Nashville: Abingdon Press, 1986), p. 68.

CHAPTER 8

xi   Adso of Montier-en-Der, "Letter on the Origin and Time of the Antichrist," trans. by Bernard McGinn, in *Apocalyptic Spirituality* (New York: Paulist Press, 1979), p. 90.

xii   Martin Luther, "A Mighty Fortress Is Our God."

CHAPTER 9

xiii   A full account of Justin's trial recorded in Acta Sancti Justini et soriorum, as translated in *A New Eusebius,* ed. by J. Stevenson (London: SPCK, 1957), pp. 28-30.

xiv   see James M. Efird, *Revelation for Today* (Nashville: Abingdon Press, 1989), p. 95.

CHAPTER 11

xv   John Wesley White, *WW III: Signs of the Impending Battle of Armageddon* (Zondervan Publishing House, 1977), p. 164.

xvi   See Grace Halsell, *Prophecy and Politics: The Secret Alliance Between Israel and the U S Christian Right* (Chicago: Chicago Review Press, 1986).

xvii   *Los Angeles Times* interview, March 4, 1981.

xviii   Robert Jewett, "Coming to Terms with the Doom Boom," *Quarterly Review* (Fall, 1984), pp. 20, 22.

xix   J.W. Bowman, "Armageddon," *Interpreter's Dictionary of the Bible,* Vol. I, p. 227.

xx   Paul Minear, *New Testament Apocalyptic* (Nashville: Abingdon Press, 1981), p. 118.

CHAPTER 12

xxi   H. Ernest Nichol, "We've a Story to Tell the Nations."

xxii   James M. Efird, *End-Times,* pp. 75-76.

xxiii   From a conversation by the author with a Jehovah's Witness in Springfield, Ohio, 1974.

CHAPTER 13

xxiv   Bruce Metzger, *Breaking the Code* (Nashville: Abingdon Press, 1993), p. 101.

xxv   G. B. Caird, *The Revelation of St John the Divine* (San Francisco: Harper & Row, 1966), p. 277.

xxvi   Bernard of Cluny, from *De Contemptu Mundi,* trans. by John Mason Neale.

CHAPTER 14

xxvii   James M. Efird, *End-Times,* p. 84.

CHAPTER 16

xxviii   Harrell F. Beck, from an address to the Ohio Pastors' Convocation, 1980.

xxix   This was an actual experience of the author during the 1980's.